T0150340

Israel Facing a New Middle East

*The Hoover Institution gratefully acknowledges
the following individuals and foundations
for their significant support of the*

HERBERT AND JANE DWIGHT WORKING GROUP
ON ISLAMISM AND THE INTERNATIONAL ORDER:

Herbert and Jane Dwight

Donald and Joan Beall
  Beall Family Foundation

S. D. Bechtel, Jr. Foundation

Lynde and Harry Bradley Foundation

Stephen and Susan Brown

Lakeside Foundation

Nancy Doyle, M.D.

HERBERT AND JANE DWIGHT WORKING GROUP ON ISLAMISM AND THE INTERNATIONAL ORDER

ISRAEL FACING A NEW MIDDLE EAST

In Search of a National Security Strategy

———————————

Itamar Rabinovich *and* Itai Brun

HOOVER INSTITUTION PRESS

STANFORD UNIVERSITY | STANFORD, CALIFORNIA

www.hoover.org

Hoover Institution Press Publication No. 678
Hoover Institution at Leland Stanford Junior University,
Stanford, California, 94305-6003

Hoover Institution Press assumes no responsibility for the persistence or accuracy
of URLs for external or third-party Internet websites referred to in this publication,
and does not guarantee that any content on such websites is, or will remain, accurate
or appropriate.

First printing 2017
24 23 22 21 20 19 18 17   9 8 7 6 5 4 3 2 1

Manufactured in the United States of America

The paper used in this publication meets the minimum requirements of the
American National Standard for Information Sciences—Permanence of Paper
for Printed Library Materials, ANSI/NISO Z39.48-1992. ♾

Cataloging-in-Publication Data is available from the Library of Congress.
ISBN 978-0-8179-2044-9 (cloth : alk. paper)
ISBN 978-0-8179-2046-3 (EPUB)
ISBN 978-0-8179-2047-0 (Mobipocket)
ISBN 978-0-8179-2048-7 (PDF)

CONTENTS

During sixty-eight years of independent statehood, Israel has fought several wars and confronted a variety of national security challenges. The Israel Defense Forces (IDF) and other components of its formidable national security establishment have on the whole performed well under the direction of successive civilian governments.

The two of us spent decades observing and studying the making of Israel's national security through our work in the IDF, Israeli diplomacy, and the academy. We were therefore delighted to be approached by Charles Hill with the idea of writing this monograph. Israel is currently contending with the challenges of the present turmoil in the Middle East equipped with a rich history of coping with military and security challenges and dramatic changes in its strategic environment. To characterize the current challenges, we decided to present briefly both the provenance of these challenges and the evolution of Israeli military-security thinking.

In this endeavor, we identified the analytical value of working at three levels: national security strategy (often referred to as "grand strategy"), the cabinet level's national security policy, and the IDF's military strategy. We were not surprised to find that for decades now, Israel has lacked a full-fledged formal grand strategy, that the cabinet's formulation of national security policy is hampered by structural and political problems, and that the IDF has played the most effective role in formulating and executing an expanded version of its mission.

Israel's national security landscape has been altered and transformed several times since 1948. In following these changes, we placed particular emphasis on two periods: the years 1979–82 (and their sequels) and the current Middle Eastern turmoil, which has exacerbated some threats facing Israel and has created new opportunities.

We both hope that this short study will encourage further discussion of the practice and theory of Israeli national strategy and national security policy and possibly also make a modest contribution toward taking advantage of the new prospects offered by this period of turmoil and change in the Middle East.

ITAMAR RABINOVICH *and* ITAI BRUN

August 2016

1

THE EVOLUTION OF ISRAEL'S NATIONAL SECURITY DOCTRINE

D ifferent nations conceptualize, formulate, and discuss national security policy in different ways. The British government publishes a comprehensive annual report on national security strategy and a strategic defense and security review. The US government publishes periodically three different reports: the president's "National Security Policy of the USA," the Pentagon's "National Defense Strategy," and the Joint Chiefs of Staff's "National Military Strategy." These two examples reflect both the looseness with which such terms as "strategy," "security," and "defense" are used and the substantive distinction among the levels of a nation's strategy or national security policy: 1) national security strategy (sometimes referred to as "grand strategy"), the formulation of the country's crucial national security interests and challenges and the broad policies pursued to protect them; 2) the government's translation of this national security strategy into national security policy (sometimes referred to as "national defense policy");

and 3) the implementation of this policy by the military leader-ship through the buildup and deployment of military force (national military strategy). Needless to say, this process and its products are not merely a top down development, but rather the outcome of ongoing interaction.

Israel is a country preoccupied, not to say obsessed, with national security challenges. It has developed formidable military and defense establishments that have been deployed over the past sixty-eight years in several wars and other military operations but has failed or chose to refrain from a systematic formulation, let alone discussion, of its grand strategy and national security policy. In Israel's case, the objective difficulty of adapting strategy to an ever-changing reality has been com-pounded by the weakness or absence of institutions entrusted with these tasks. Israel's original grand strategy was formu-lated by its founding father, David Ben Gurion, in his dual capacity as prime minister and minister of defense. The "Secu-rity Review" that he presented to his cabinet in October 1953 was, as will be shown below, a remarkable document. It underlay Israel's national security policy through the Six-Day War in June 1967. The massive changes generated by that war and subsequent developments confronted Israel with new chal-lenges and opportunities and produced a series of changes in Israel's national security doctrine and practice. Over the years, several initiatives were taken to reformulate Israel's national security doctrine. Most were not completed. Three of them, the Meridor Commission report and Chief of Staff Halutz's docu-ment in 2006 (both made available to the public), as well as *The IDF Strategy*, published by the IDF's chief of general staff Gadi Eizenkot in 2015, will be reviewed and analyzed below.

But these reports did not seek to formulate and present a full-fledged grand strategy comparable to Ben Gurion's 1953 security review. (These documents, it should be noted, were written at different levels. The Halutz and Eizenkot documents deal with the IDF's operational concept, while the Meridor report had a more ambitious scope.) This may seem odd given the numerous transformations of Israel's national security environment and policies over time, but those familiar with Israel's political culture will not be surprised by the fact that, as in other areas, its political and military leaders chose time and again to update the country's national security policy in a piecemeal way rather than formulate and articulate a comprehensive new policy.

Furthermore, as this study will demonstrate, the three levels of strategy described above have not been applied by Israel's political and military leadership over the years. Ben Gurion's grand strategy as formulated in 1953 stands out as a solitary effort. Subsequent leaders took steps that can be placed at the grand strategy level (Yitzhak Rabin in 1992, Shimon Peres in 1995, Ehud Barak in 1999, Ariel Sharon in 2005, and Ehud Olmert in 2008), but such measures did not match the ambitious, comprehensive grand strategy formulated by Ben Gurion. The policy adopted by right-wing leaders after 1967, which sought either to perpetuate the status quo or to achieve a de facto annexation of the West Bank can be described as a grand strategy of sorts in that it has aimed to shape Israel's destiny by failing to make explicit choices. More recently, the radical right wing, which is currently represented in the government and the security cabinet, has been advocating a proactive agenda to annex the West Bank or at least part of it.

In practice, Israel's strategy and defense policy has been largely conducted at the level of national security policy, as policies were pursued and decisions made by prime ministers, defense ministers, and the IDF leadership. Moreover, the boundary between national security policy and military strategy has been blurred by the weakness of the national defense strategy level and by the effectiveness of the IDF leadership in planning and advocating for a strategy. The Israeli governmental system has lacked a mechanism at the cabinet level to formulate and implement an effective national security policy. The Ministerial National Security Committee (the security/political cabinet, a relatively new entity) has failed to function as an effective body. The National Security Council has not been empowered by successive prime ministers, and the Ministry of Defense lacks the resources to play this role. The IDF, by contrast, possesses highly qualified personnel, a powerful military intelligence, and an efficient planning division, and has enjoyed popular credibility and prestige, which have turned the IDF as a whole and its chief of staff, in particular, into powerful actors beyond the military and strategic realms. Consequently, the Israeli system has operated over the years on two of the three levels of national strategy, and oftentimes on one, namely the uninstitutionalized interaction between the cabinet level and the IDF. In fact, the most crucial axis has typically been the informal relationship among the prime minister, the minister of defense, and the IDF chief of staff, occasionally supplemented by the heads of the security services.

The first part of this monograph will introduce Israel's original grand strategy, national security policy, and military strategy. The second part will review and analyze the changes they underwent in the aftermath of June 1967, as well as subsequent developments into the 1990s. The third and most important part will deal with the radical changes in both challenges and responses that led to and are reflected the Second Lebanon War and the three campaigns in Gaza and are addressed in the Meridor, Halutz, and Eizenkot documents. We argue that profound and dramatic as developments in the Middle East in recent years have been, Israel has in fact been coping not so much with novel security challenges but with developments that have reinforced trends whose roots go back to the early 1980s. The fourth part will examine the options available to Israel in the current circumstances and will elaborate on the functioning of the different levels of its strategy.

DAVID BEN GURION'S SECURITY REVIEW

In October 1953, Israel's prime minister and minister of defense, David Ben Gurion, presented to his cabinet a comprehensive security review, known as "The Military and the State." The review was prepared during a three-month leave that Ben Gurion took to conduct a thorough study of Israel's security position. He decided to conduct this study when he became aware of the IDF's poor state and concerned about its ability to respond to the country's massive security challenges. Ben Gurion's study was facilitated by senior officers from the IDF's General Headquarters (GHQ).

The Israeli leader's point of departure was that the Arab states defeated in the 1948 war had not accepted their defeat and were determined to complete the task they had failed to accomplish in 1948. Ben Gurion realized that Israel had no prospect of inflicting a decisive military defeat on the Arab states and bringing the conflict to an end through military victory. The Arabs could sustain multiple defeats and needed just one victory to destroy the Jewish state. The demographic disparity and the difference in resources were such that over time the Arabs could acquire the weapon systems and military capacity they had lacked in 1948 (and still lacked in 1953), thus presenting Israel with an insurmountable challenge. But Israel had several advantages that it could maximize. Its small territory denied it strategic depth but gave it the advantage of short internal lines and the ability to move troops swiftly from one front to the other. Israel had better qualified manpower, enjoyed superior ethos and solidarity, and was a single actor, in contrast to the disunited Arab world.

To maximize these advantages, Ben Gurion wanted to expand Israel's population, increase recruitment to the military, develop an efficient intelligence service, and create an air force that could play a major role in improving Israel's strategic position vis-à-vis its Arab enemies. Ben Gurion saw national security as an integrated system in which the IDF was part of a larger whole. Israel of the early 1950s was a poor country that could hardly afford to maintain a large army or buy expensive weapons systems—which, in any event, were not easily available. His solution was to keep the IDF as a relatively small force composed of a small standing army reinforced by compulsory national service, and to rely on a sophisticated system of reserves that would be called up in the event of imminent war. A mobilized society, a massive educational effort among the country's youth, and a limited military budget were some of the elements designated to make the IDF part of a larger national effort rather than an autonomous entity. Israel was during that period "a nation in uniform." Ben Gurion's point of departure was pessimistic in that he assumed the Arabs would not come to terms with Israel's existence and would continue hostilities even after multiple defeats. But he did expect that at the end of the day, after having failed to defeat Israel, their leadership might conclude that they had to accept Israel. In this respect, Ben Gurion accepted the concept if not the term coined by his political rival, Ze'ev Jabotinsky, "the Iron Wall": the notion that if the Jewish state managed to build an iron wall that the Arabs could not bring down, they would end up accepting it.

From these points of departure came the three foundations of Israel's national strategy (they were adopted in practice prior to being conceptualized): general deterrence, early warning, and decisive victory. Since Israel could not expect to prevent the Arabs from attacking, it could at least make these wars less frequent. This could be achieved by general deterrence, which in turn depended on decisive victories. In other words, by defeating Arab enemies, Israel would convince them to delay a new attack as long as the effect of the last defeat was still fresh. And given that the Arab states had standing armies and could launch wars quite easily, Israel needed an efficient intelligence system to have sufficient early warning to mobilize the reserves, the main fighting force of the IDF. And once war broke out, since

Israel had no strategic depth, it had to shift the war into enemy territory. Given the cost of war to a country relying largely on reserves, wars had to be brought to a swift conclusion by a decisive military victory, which would, at the same time, enhance deterrence. This approach could easily be perceived as offensive, but in essence it was a defensive policy. Israel was interested in minimizing wars, and the offensive strategy adopted once war seemed imminent or inevitable was essentially preventive and defensive.

These principles were supplemented, in Ben Gurion's view of national security, by three additional elements. The first was the quest for an alliance with a major power. Such an alliance could provide Israel with sophisticated weapons systems and offer protection of Israel's skies in the event of war. The second was what came to be known as "the Dimona project" or "nuclear ambiguity," which was to provide Israel with the ultimate guarantee against Arab ambitions to destroy it. Whatever the Dimona project was in reality, the Arab perception that Israel possessed a nuclear weapon provided effective deterrence. A close alliance with France in the mid-1950s provided Israel with weapons systems, aerial defense during the 1956 war, and nuclear technology. Israel's defense pact with France was supplemented in the 1950s and early 1960s by more limited defense cooperation with West Germany. Ben Gurion was naturally interested in a close political and military relationship with the United States, but Washington was not interested prior to the June 1967 war. President Kennedy agreed in 1962 to provide Israel with Hawk antiaircraft missiles, which were defined as a defensive system. A third element was the effort to overcome

Arab hostility by cultivating relations with other minorities in the region and by leapfrogging over the immediate circle of hostile Arab states to develop an "alliance of the periphery" with Turkey, Iran, and Ethiopia, who all shared a hostility to radical Arab nationalism and Soviet policy in the Middle East.

During the 1950s and 1960s the IDF developed the principles of its operational doctrine. In the 1948 war, the IDF's ground forces were composed primarily of infantry supplemented by mobile elements: jeeps, armored cars, and light tanks. The air force consisted of a small number of diverse airplanes. In line with Ben Gurion's thinking, the IDF was built as a small regular army supplemented by a large reserve army, and ground maneuver was placed at the center of the operational doctrine. To enable an effective ground maneuver, it was decided to build the IDF as a mobile mechanized army capable of quickly switching from defense to offense, taking advantage of internal lines to win on one front while conducting a defensive war on the other fronts. The construction of the reserve army was inspired by the Swiss example of a reserve army kept at adequate professional levels through annual training and capable of being swiftly mobilized and deployed. But unlike the Swiss system, the Israeli reserve army includes mostly ground forces, while the air force and navy rely on career officers, NCOs, and draftees.

The IDF had sound reasons to allocate a central role to the ground forces and ground maneuver. The main threat to Israel came from the enemy's ground forces. The common political perception was that the conflict with the Arabs was essentially territorial, and it followed that the territorial dimension on both sides of the border was particularly significant. The strategic-military concept emphasized shifting the war to enemy territory, a result of the lack of strategic depth and the need for a swift and visible victory. These considerations naturally led Israelis to emphasize capturing enemy territory and destroying its forces, and then to the conclusion that the dominant element in obtaining military victory was the ground maneuver. The centrality of ground maneuver in the IDF's original operational concept was reinforced by its potential to take advantage of the quality of Israeli forces and to minimize the enemy's quantitative advantage. The IDF leadership saw as optimal a dynamic ground maneuver conducted under rapidly changing conditions, requiring the army at all levels to display initiative, flexibility, coordination, and adaptation to new and unexpected conditions.

THE SINAI CAMPAIGN

When writing his security review in 1953, Ben Gurion was prescient. He predicted war in about three years and pointed to the possible rise of a charismatic Arab leader capable of mobilizing the Arab world in an unprecedented way. Indeed, the rise of Gamal Abdel Nasser as the messianic leader of Egypt and the Arab world in 1954 presented Israel with severe challenges. From 1948 until Nasser's arrival on the scene, the Arab world shared a desire to reverse the consequences of the 1948 war but had no coherent plan to achieve this aim. Nasser's idea was that the State of Israel could be liquidated only by regular military forces launching a comprehensive war against the Jewish state. But Nasser realized that the Arab armies were not up to the task and that it would take time for them to develop adequate capability.

Nasser's alliance with the Soviet Union, the massive Czech-Egyptian arms deal of 1955, the wave of terrorism launched by Egypt from the Gaza Strip and the West Bank, and the closure of the Red Sea to Israeli shipping led the Israeli leadership to adopt the notion of a preemptive war. Israel's decision to launch the Sinai campaign reflected the ultimate failure of its policy of retaliation. Arab terrorism from the West Bank and the Gaza Strip led to a series of "retaliatory operations" against Jordanian and Egyptian targets, predicated on the assumption that the responsibility for anti-Israeli operations lay with the host government, whether it initiated such operations (Egypt) or failed to prevent them (Jordan). These operations had run their course by 1956. Nasser's conflict with Great Britain and France created an opportunity for Israeli collaboration with these two declining colonial powers and led to the combined Suez-Sinai War of 1956. While the larger Suez operation was inspired by an outdated reading of the regional and international environments and ended in failure, Israel's military campaign in Sinai was a great success. Israel's decisive victory over the Egyptian army in the Sinai reinforced its deterrence and led to a period of relative calm that lasted eleven years.

The IDF's offensive doctrine was shaped in the decade that followed the Sinai campaign by the lessons of that war. The abstract notions of ground maneuver and shifting the conflict to enemy territory were applied successfully during the Sinai campaign. The war demonstrated that the reserve army could be mobilized and deployed to penetrate enemy territory and destroy forces with limited casualties. The centrality of ground maneuver and the dominance of armored forces were reflected in the composition of the IDF's senior command, which was made up primarily of senior ground forces officers. This, however, did not preclude development of Israel's air force. It had been seen from an early stage as a cardinal component of Israel's military might. The underlying concept was of a standing air force, readily available and flexible, capable of defending the country's airspace, achieving aerial superiority, and offering tactical support to the ground forces. This was supplemented by the perception that the air force also had a role on the strategic level, primarily in attacking national infrastructure (economic as well as military) deep in enemy territory, thus enhancing deterrence. The Israeli model, as it developed during these years, continues to give the air force a great deal of independence and a direct approach to the political level while it remains subordinated to the General Staff and overall military strategy.

Until the spring of 1967, Nasser acted consistently under the assumption that Arab armies were still not ready for a comprehensive war against Israel. But Nasser's approach was challenged from two directions. One was the emergence of young Palestinians who had lost faith in the Arab states' ability and perhaps willingness to defeat Israel. These young Palestinians established the Fatah organization in the late 1950s to launch military and terrorist operations against Israel. The other was the Syrian Baathist doctrine of the "popular war of liberation." Nasser's Baathist rivals argued that his strategy amounted to acceptance of Israel and contended that the lesson of Vietnam showed that a strategy of "popular war" modeled after the Vietcong could defeat the might of the IDF. The actions taken by Fatah and the Syrian Baath regime and Israel's responses produced the crisis of May 1967, which led to the Six-Day War.

THE SIX-DAY WAR

The Six-Day War of June 1967 was a watershed. In May 1967 Israel faced one of the most severe crises in its history. It emerged from that crisis with a spectacular military victory. In the course of six days, it defeated the Egyptian, Syrian, and Jordanian armies and an Iraqi expeditionary force and captured large territories in the Sinai, the Golan Heights, and the West Bank. In military terms, the Six-Day War displayed an almost perfect implementation of the IDF's operational doctrine of the late 1950s and early 1960s: the Israeli Air Force used preemptive strikes to destroy the Egyptian, Syrian, and Jordanian air forces on the ground, and IDF tanks effectively implemented the ground maneuver.

The war turned Israel into a major regional power, established the IDF's reputation as one of the world's best military forces, and laid the foundation for a new close relationship with the United States. But it also created new challenges and placed the future of the newly occupied territories at the center of Israel's national agenda and debate. Israel initially offered to return the Sinai Peninsula and the Golan Heights to Egypt and Syria in return for full-fledged peace agreements and adequate security arrangements. There was no such offer with regard to the West Bank and the Gaza Strip, which were seen as part of historic Palestine, or the Land of Israel. During the following months and years, peace with Egypt and Syria did not come. With regard to the West Bank and the Gaza Strip, a powerful messianic movement emerged seeking to preserve Israeli control over the whole of the Land of Israel, eventually becoming a powerful force in Israeli politics. These developments, as well as the Arabs' initial refusal to accept the defeat and agree to a peaceful resolution of the conflict, created a new situation in which for the first time since the end of the British Mandate in 1948, the whole of historic Palestine was under one rule, and Israel controlled a large Palestinian population within its borders (the Arab minority in Israel proper and the Palestinian population in the West Bank and Gaza).

The collapse of Israeli deterrence in May 1967 and the prospect of a collective Arab effort to surround Israel with three hostile Arab armies under Egyptian command led many Israelis to argue that the country, as defined by the boundaries of the armistice agreements of 1949, was indefensible. This sense was reinforced by Washington's reluctance during the crisis of May 1967 to live up to the commitments made by President Eisenhower in 1957, when he pressured Israel to withdraw from the Sinai Peninsula. Consequently, a security argument reinforced the ideological attachment to Greater Israel and fueled the argument for retaining all or most of the territories captured in June 1967. In the aftermath of the stunning 1967 victory, Israel's political and military leadership, intoxicated by the magnitude of the victory, underestimated Egyptian and Syrian determination to regain their occupied national territory and failed to adapt IDF strategy to the new geopolitical realities.

Israel's original national security strategy, national defense strategy, and national military strategy were all transformed by these developments. The original consensus over Israel's most important concern—Arab determination to destroy the Jewish state—was replaced by an ongoing debate between those who believed Israel should seek a political settlement with the Arabs on the basis of minor modifications of the 1949 lines, internationally guaranteed peace treaties, and security arrangements, and those who sought to retain the territories captured in June 1967 as the best guarantee of Israel's national security.

Between 1967 and 1973, Israel had to contend with new challenges under new conditions. The familiar advantage of short internal lines was replaced by deployment over long distances, from the Golan Heights in the north to the banks of the Suez Canal in the south. A country that had no strategic depth between 1949 and 1967 came to possess significant depth, particularly in the Sinai. Israel could have defended the Sinai by taking advantage of this depth and deploying a mobile armored force there. But habit prevailed, and the IDF leadership chose to build the Bar-Lev Line along the Suez Canal.

THE WAR OF ATTRITION

Israel had to deal with a new form of warfare, a "war of attrition" launched by Egypt and joined by Syria and eventually the Palestine Liberation Organization (PLO), as well as a new level of terrorism launched by the PLO and other Palestinian groups. The concept of attrition reflected an Arab perception that Israel, being particularly sensitive to casualties, would find it difficult over time to pay the price exacted by Arab rivals much more tolerant of casualties. The IDF also found it difficult to deal with a form of warfare that was stationary in nature, required the maintenance of strict routine, and ran against the grain of the IDF's ethos of dynamism and forward movement.

As the war of attrition with Egypt escalated and Israel began deep bombing raids in Egypt, the Soviet Union dispatched air defense systems, and eventually warplanes, in Egypt's defense. For the first time, Israel found itself in a military confrontation with the Soviet Union. Inside Israel, the consensus over national security policy began to erode as many young Israelis questioned the necessity of casualties, arguing that a political settlement predicated on territorial concessions was available.

THE OCTOBER WAR OF 1973

On October 6, 1973, Israel was surprised by a coordinated attack launched by Egypt and Syria in the Sinai and the Golan Heights. The war's initial phase saw major achievements for the Egyptian and Syrian armies. The Egyptian army successfully crossed the Suez Canal, captured most of the Bar-Lev Line, and established itself on the canal's eastern bank. The Syrian army recaptured most of the Golan Heights and threatened to advance toward Israel proper. The intelligence surprise and the political leadership's decision to refrain from a preemptive strike created a situation whereby during the first few days, before the reserve units were successfully deployed, the IDF found itself in an inferior position on both fronts. It also turned out that with ground-to-air missiles and antitank tactical missiles, the Egyptian and Syrian armies were able to neutralize the superiority of Israel's air force and armored units. It took several days and heavy casualties before the IDF regrouped and moved to the offensive. By the war's end, Israel had been able to recapture the whole of the Golan Heights and threaten Damascus. In addition, the army had crossed the Suez Canal, encircled the Egyptian Third Army, and was on the verge of inflicting a major defeat on Egypt.

The October War was seen in Israel as "an earthquake" due to the intelligence failure, the IDF's poor performance in early phases of the war, and the heavy casualties. One of the war's most important consequences was the launching of an Egyptian-Israeli peace process that culminated in the 1979 peace treaty between the two countries. In terms of military doctrine, rather than undermining the IDF's traditional outlook, the war led to a reinforcement of the centrality of ground maneuver and the air force. IDF ground forces were increased; the number of tanks grew by 50 percent, artillery by 100 percent, and armored personnel carriers (APC) by 800 percent. The air force was increased by 40 percent, and its leadership became preoccupied with finding an effective strategy to destroy or neutralize ground-to-air missiles. In tactical terms, greater emphasis was put on integrating armored units with infantry so that infantry units could neutralize the enemy's antitank missiles.

Another important outcome of the October War was a dramatic decline in the Israeli public's trust in the traditional political and military leadership. It led, four years later, to the first transfer of power from Labor to the right wing, and resulted over the next three decades in greater willingness on the part of the Israeli public and politicians to question and challenge the leadership's position on national security issues.

THE ISRAELI-EGYPTIAN PEACE

The Israeli-Egyptian peace treaty in 1979 was a dramatic turning point in Israel's history and its national security position. Ben Gurion's original concept was vindicated when an Egyptian leader came to the conclusion, after several rounds of war, that his country could no longer pay the price of conflict with Israel and was willing to sign a full-fledged peace agreement. The 1979 treaty was the culmination of a peace process that began in the aftermath of the October War, and it was made possible by Anwar Sadat's leadership in Egypt. On the Israeli side, it represented the kind of a radical change of perspective that radical political change can produce. Menachem Begin had been an outsider, an opposition leader for thirty years. But when he became prime minister, he jettisoned an important part of his traditional outlook and made a radical decision: Israel would withdraw from the Sinai in return for full peace and a satisfactory security regime in the region. The Israeli-Egyptian peace was the first implementation of the concept of "land for peace": Egypt would regain the entire Sinai in return for full contractual peace and an adequate security regime in the Sinai. Fortunately, the Sinai Peninsula could serve as a security barrier between the two countries, providing the basis for a mutually acceptable security regime. Egypt's departure from the "Arab circle of hostility" represented a significant improvement in Israel's overall security position. It also was the first major crack in the post-1948 Arab strategy of delegitimizing and boycotting Israel in anticipation of another round of fighting. The peace treaty with Egypt and the first opportunity for a large number of Israelis to visit a major Arab country prompted Israeli policy makers, analysts, and intellectuals to start grappling with the prospect of integrating Israel into the Middle Eastern environment. This was a significant departure from one of the original tenets of Ben Gurion's grand strategy, which assumed that the Arab world would persist for a long time in its rejection of Israel. Egypt's decision to keep a "cold peace" with Israel limited the impact of the peace agreement on the Israeli public and kept discussion of potential integration into the region at the margins of the Israeli public discourse.

THE 1980S GROUND MANEUVER CRISIS

Several developments, including the 1982 war with Lebanon, converged in the early 1980s to generate a debate within Israel on the value and relevance of one of the hallowed foundations of Israel's military strategy: the ground maneuver.

The 1982 War in Lebanon

The controversial 1982 war in Lebanon produced bitter controversy and a lively debate in Israel over political and military aspects of its national security policies.

As we saw, the October War of 1973 undermined the Israeli public's overwhelming support for the civilian and military custodians of national security. The Sinai Campaign was in the strict sense "a war of choice," but it was not seen as such by an Israeli public living under siege; by contrast, the war in Lebanon was increasingly seen as an illegitimate use of the IDF to implement a political programme. The debate between Right and Left was fueled by a growing sense that the government, minister of defense Ariel Sharon in particular, had misled the public, as well as by the massacre perpetrated by Israel's Lebanese allies in the Palestinian refugee camps of Sabra and Shatila. The public anger erupted in a huge demonstration that led to the formation of a second judicial commission of inquiry within a decade and to Sharon's removal from the Ministry of Defense.

Israel's Peace for the Galilee operation, as it was officially named, was motivated and shaped by two entirely different sets of considerations. One goal, as the official name implied, was to remove the threat presented by Palestinian organizations that had turned Lebanon into their main base after being expelled from Jordan. Menachem Begin's government was hard put to contend with the terrorist raids launched into Israel from South Lebanon and with the Katyusha rockets fired across the border. The artillery duel between the IDF and the PLO in July 1981, which ended inconclusively, was an important milestone in persuading the Israeli leadership to be more radical in dealing with this challenge. But at a deeper level lay Defense Minister Sharon's bold vision of transforming Israel's strategic position through an alliance with the Lebanese Forces militia and the Phalange Party. The joint plan was to destroy the PLO's "state within a state" in Lebanon, to expel the Syrian forces that had entered Lebanon in 1976, to elect Bashir Gemayel as Lebanon's new president, and to induce Lebanon to sign a peace agreement with Israel. Israel would then have a peace agreement with a second Arab state. Needless to say, it was a house of cards that collapsed soon after the war's end. Menachem Begin, who realized in 1981 that his gamble on a separate peace with Egypt had failed, was willing to go along. But the failure of the "grand plan" and the public's realization that they had been misled by Sharon and possibly Begin produced an unusually sharp reaction.

One curious flaw in the concept that underlay the Lebanon War was the ill-fated partnership with the Phalange Party. It was an egregious manifestation of the pre-state and early-state tendency to seek partnerships with other minority groups in the region in order to find cracks in the Arab nationalist wall of hostility. The 1979 peace treaty with Egypt represented the first real crack in that wall and could have been used as the starting point of an entirely different strategy. The choice made by Begin and Sharon was a blow to that option.

With regard to military strategy, the Lebanon War represented the IDF's lingering attachment to its original operational doctrine. Israel invaded Lebanon with a large ground force and conducted relatively successful battles with PLO forces in the western and central sectors and with the Syrians in the eastern sector. But a difference was clear in the implementation of ground maneuver. The enhanced sensitivity to casualties evident since the October 1973 War led to more careful conduct of ground maneuver and limited its effectiveness. This led also to greater reliance on firepower as an increasingly important component of Israel's offensive strategy.

The Debate on the Original Operational Concept

The Lebanon War contributed in two ways to the 1980s debate on the relevance of the IDF's traditional emphasis on ground maneuver and the offensive approach. The difficulties encountered in moving the IDF's tanks in mountainous terrain and in penetrating Syrian defenses in the eastern sector raised questions as to the centrality of the tank to Israel's military strategy, the prospect of replacing it to some extent with the attack helicopter and other novel technologies, and the usefulness of the offensive approach as opposed to greater reliance on defense. The debate derived from developments in Israel and its strategic environment but was also nourished by the ripple effects of a similar debate in the United States.

These developments served also as a backdrop for the growing effectiveness and operational importance of Israel's air force. The air force drew the correct lessons from the October War and applied them effectively. In 1982 it destroyed Syria's ground-to-air missiles and a large number of Syrian warplanes; it also used its mastery of Lebanon's airspace to support the ground forces. In 1981, when it destroyed Iraq's nuclear reactor, and in 1985, when it attacked the PLO headquarters in Tunis, it displayed Israel's ability to project power. Armed with growing amounts of precision-guided munitions, it helped create the sense that aerial warfare was different, more precise, more effective, and less costly in lives. This perception eventually led to a change in the IDF's original operational concept.

The war in Lebanon was significant in yet another way. It was the first war Israel had waged after signing the peace treaty with Egypt. The durability of this peace treaty was tested by the conduct of a war waged in the territory of another Arab state, but the peace treaty as such was not affected.

Lebanon's Long-Term Impact

The Lebanon War failed to achieve most of its ambitious goals, but it did result in the PLO's departure from Lebanon to a new base in Tunisia. What the war's authors did not expect was the PLO leadership's decision six years later, as a result of this turn of events, to change its strategy and agree to a negotiated settlement with Israel.

There were also two negative consequences. One was an eighteen-year-long Israeli deployment in Lebanon. Israel withdrew from the environs of Beirut to a security zone north of its border with Lebanon but could not bring itself to withdraw completely from Lebanon until 2000. It was a costly mistake that exacted high casualties and other costs. The IDF soldiers were the targets of an effective guerilla war conducted by a new Shiite militia, Hezbollah, which, with Iranian and Syrian support, built its reputation and prestige by fighting the IDF.

Hezbollah's development was part of a larger—and, from Israel's perspective, ominous—development: the projection of Iran's Islamic Revolution and new regional ambitions from the region's eastern margin into the core area of the Middle East. This might well have happened in any event, but Israel's invasion of Lebanon and its continuing presence in the mainly Shiite south facilitated the process. Together with its Syrian allies, Iran introduced suicide bombings and built Hezbollah as a hybrid entity—a terrorist organization, a militia, a political movement, and ultimately an arm of the Iranian regime. Hezbollah gradually came to dominate the Shiite community and became the strongest force in Lebanon, surpassing the state and the army. Iran thus established itself on Israel's northern border as a direct participant in the Arab-Israeli conflict, providing Hezbollah with a massive arsenal of rockets and missiles as a deterrent to Israeli action.

2

NEW CHALLENGES FOR
ISRAEL'S NATIONAL SECURITY

THE EVOLUTION OF THE OPERATIONAL
CONCEPT OF THE "OTHER SIDE"

The 1980s

Between 1979 and 1982 a series of developments converged to set in motion a process that culminated over the coming years in a new set of security challenges to Israel.

The single most important development was the Islamic Revolution in Iran. Like other major revolutions, the Iranian Revolution sought to export itself. Its natural constituencies were the Shiite communities in the Middle East, first and foremost in Lebanon. Iran's new regime built a strategic partnership with Syria, a country dominated by a sectarian Shiite minority that shared Iran's rivalry with Iraq and held sway in Lebanon. Together they brought into the equation suicide bombing and Hezbollah's arsenal of rockets and missiles. Iran's entry into the Middle Eastern political system was also a major development. A successor state to empires that had dominated large parts of the region, Iran had played a marginal role in the region during most of the twentieth century because it was preoccupied with the Soviet challenge and domestic problems. The injection into the region of a regional power with a large population, an oil economy, and a sophisticated elite was a significant development. For eight years its influence was blunted by a war with Iraq, but war also prompted the two sides to escalate their military capacities. The trauma of the war motivated Iran to invest huge resources in developing its strategic potential, with a particular emphasis on weapons of mass destruction and ballistic missiles. Iran's new leaders came to understand the importance of military organization and professionalism, adding to its traditional emphasis on religious devotion. The war had a comparable effect on Iraq's military doctrine and buildup as they were manifested during the First Gulf War and the subsequent decade.

Another significant event in 1979 was the Soviet invasion of Afghanistan, which added two other dimensions to the Afghan civil war: a national war of liberation against foreign occupation and, for the Islamist element, a holy war, jihad. In time the anti-Soviet forces were reinforced by external support and an influx of volunteers from across the Muslim world. The defeat of the Soviet Union provided the mujahideen with a narrative of victory and helped build a generation of highly qualified and highly motivated fighters. Al-Qaeda, which was founded toward the end of the decade, was a distinctive product of these developments.

The Israeli-Syrian strategic equation underwent important changes during those years. The Israeli-Egyptian peace treaty left Syria exposed. Syria sustained a major blow during the 1982 Lebanon War, when its hegemonic position in Lebanon was severely threatened. But over time Syria rebuilt its position and, in cooperation with Iran, transformed its Lebanese assets into a major advantage. In the early 1980s Syria was faced with a right-wing Israeli government that in 1981 destroyed Iraq's nuclear reactor and launched the Lebanon War. The Reagan administration was critical of the destruction of the Iraqi nuclear reactor, but in November 1981 the United States and Israel signed a strategic memorandum of understanding, manifesting the special relationship between the two countries, particularly in the defense/strategic area. To Middle Eastern actors like Syria, Iran, and the PLO, this was proof enough that the United States and Israel were acting together to promote common strategic goals and relying on similar weapons systems. Israel's destruction of the Iraqi nuclear reactor was a manifestation of a new policy (known as the Begin Doctrine), according to which Israel would not allow any hostile Middle Eastern state to possess nuclear military capability. But to enemies like Syria, the attack demonstrated Israel's ability to project power precisely and effectively over great distances and to act decisively when its national security interests were threatened.

Relying on Soviet support, Hafez al-Assad launched a policy of seeking strategic parity with Israel. The economic costs of this effort were prohibitive and motivated Syria to look for alternative strategies in its effort to overcome Israel's technological superiority.

In retrospect, the years 1979–82 can be seen as the period of turmoil that eventually led to the development of the other side's operational concept. The IDF was busy redeploying after withdrawing from the Sinai and was preparing for a potential war on the northern border. Its preparations reflected, as we can now see, its attachment to the prevailing strategic concept and failure to understand the full significance of the turmoil in the region.

The 1990s

The consequences and repercussions of the dramatic events of 1979–82 were clearly visible in the 1980s and came to a head during the transition to the next decade. Indeed, during the early 1990s the foundations were laid for ideas that ripened "on the other side" into a coherent concept designed to provide an adequate response to the technological superiority attributed to the United States but also to Israel. In the early 1990s the collapse of the Soviet Union was a fait accompli. The main Arab armies, customers of Soviet doctrine and weapon systems, were deeply impressed by the display of US military power during the First Gulf War. These armies found themselves in the midst of a severe crisis that forced them to fundamentally change their strategic and operational concepts. These changes were particularly evident in Syria and Iran.

The Soviet Union's collapse led to the collapse of Syria's national security plan. There was no longer a Soviet umbrella to protect from Israeli or American threats. The Syrian leadership became preoccupied with the strategic implications of the precise weapon systems possessed by the United States and Israel. They were first exposed to them in 1982, when the Israeli Air Force effectively destroyed Syria's surface-to-air missiles in Lebanon, operating beyond their range and relying on electronic warfare. Later in the 1980s the Syrians were intensely busy trying to master new methods of coping with precision-guided munition with the help of Soviet advisers, who shared their need to cope with the threat that was evolving in the West. But it was Syrian participation in the US-led coalition in the First Gulf War that fully exposed the country's military leadership to the full scope of the novel technologies available to Western armies.

Iran emerged exhausted from eight years of war with Iraq. A difficult economic situation, failures on the battlefield, and the population's low morale (largely due to the missiles launched at Tehran in 1988) led its leadership to accept an Iraqi offer to end the war. About half of its weapons were destroyed during the war, and replenishing stockpiles proved to be difficult. Much of the weaponry procured in the course of the war, primarily from China and other communist countries, consisted of outdated models.

In the war's aftermath, Iranian efforts to re-arm were constrained by budgetary limitations and by US pressure on several countries to refrain from selling to Iran. In 1991 Iran did not take part in the Gulf War but did watch it closely. The conclusions it drew reinforced the lessons of the war with Iraq. The technological superiority of Western armies was clear, leading them to conclude that their country needed unconventional weapons to contend with this superiority.

THE RISE OF THE ORGANIZATIONS

During the first half of the 1990s Iran and Syria could take some comfort in several developments. Both benefited from Iraq's defeat in the First Gulf War. Syria managed to rebuild its position in Lebanon, to emerge from its economic crisis, and to improve its diplomatic position by participating in the US-led coalition and joining the new Madrid (Arab-Israeli) peace process. Yet on the whole, given the Soviet Union's collapse and Washington's ascendancy, both countries felt besieged and under pressure.

It is against this backdrop that the new prominence of three organizations founded in the 1980s should be seen. These organizations took the lead in fighting the United States and Israel in the 1990s and during the first decade of the new century.

Hezbollah was founded in Lebanon in late 1982 and came to prominence in late 1983 through a series of terrorist attacks that led US and French forces to depart Lebanon in the spring of 1984. In 1985 Israel too withdrew to the security belt in South Lebanon. In the 1980s Hezbollah competed with the Amal Movement for control of Lebanon's Shiite community, but closer cooperation between Iran and Syria led Syria (Amal's patron) to reduce the organization's profile and allow Hezbollah to take the lead in the struggle against Israel's presence in South Lebanon. During the 1980s Hezbollah, with Iran's help, built an extensive network of social and welfare services as one way of consolidating its control of a large area in southern and eastern Lebanon and in South Beirut. Since 1992 the organization has added a political dimension to its activity and has represented the bulk of the Shiite community in Lebanon's parliament.

Hamas was founded in the Gaza Strip in December 1987, shortly after the outbreak of the First Intifada. Hamas views itself as the Palestinian branch of the Egyptian Muslim Brotherhood. It defines itself as an Islamist and more radical alternative to the PLO and has resorted to terrorism, in contrast to the PLO's drift toward a political path. Like its parent organization in Egypt, Hamas operates a network of social services. Hamas was unintentionally helped by the Israeli government, which in response to its terrorist acts deported several hundred Hamas activists to Lebanon in December 1992. Israel later had to take them back, but their stay in Lebanon endowed the organization with a degree of cohesion it had not possessed earlier. Hamas's position as a rival to the PLO was also bolstered by the ties its militants established with Hezbollah and the Iranian Revolutionary Guards during their stay in Lebanon.

Al-Qaeda was founded in 1988 and grew out of an organization called the Bureau of Services, which absorbed and managed the thousands of Muslim volunteers who arrived in Afghanistan to support the local mujahideen in their conflict with the Soviet Union. The organization's three founding fathers, Osama bin Laden, Ayman al-Zawahiri, and Abdullah Azzam, arrived in Afghanistan in the years 1979–80. For the three men, the war in Afghanistan that ended in 1989 was a formative experience—as it was for a whole generation of young Muslims. They saw the mujahideen's victory over the Soviet empire as a victory of values and culture, proof of their ability to contend with complex military challenges. Their campaign created a broad base of volunteers armed with religious passion and military experience, and ready to propagate radical jihadi ideas. In the eyes of many Muslims, the Soviet Union's collapse shortly after its defeat in Afghanistan was a direct result of that war.

A NEW OPERATIONAL CONCEPT

The term "the end of history" gained currency during this period as an appropriate reflection of the optimistic sense in the West (and in Israel) that the Soviet Union's collapse and the end of the Cold War would usher in a new era, one characterized by the ascendancy of democratic and free-market ideologies, globalization, and peace shaped by the quest for prosperity. These ideas were not received with the same enthusiasm in the Middle East, where a different interpretation of the realities of these years led to the formulation of a new strategy and a new way of waging war.

The new operational concept was the product of an acute crisis and limited choices. The same reality that bred an optimistic mood in the West and in Israel was interpreted in an entirely different fashion. This new concept was formulated by leaders, commanders, and fighters in the Middle East, who acted on the basis of their heritage, culture, and observation of the military operations of the 1990s. Particularly significant was their understanding of the social and political developments of the 1990s, when their rivals, the United States and Israel in particular, were forced to conduct what David Halberstam called "war in time of peace."

Thus a concept of warfare developed according to which, alongside the technological superiority of one party, balance and equality might exist in other areas, thus reversing the disequilibrium. This concept is predicated on the assumption that the technologically challenged party to the conflict might have an advantage in areas such as the size of its territory and population. Furthermore, this concept attaches great importance to differences in the interests at stake, war aims, determination, endurance, willingness to take risks, and sensitivity to casualties. The technologically challenged party can sometimes be free of political and cultural constraints that limit the technologically superior adversary.

Since the 1990s, Israel's (and Washington's) rivals have engaged in an intensive effort to translate three major insights into action:

1) The need to significantly improve their capacity to absorb and survive in order to have the staying power required to confront modern armies. They fully understood the deadly effect of two capabilities possessed by their adversaries: precision-guided munition and novel intelligence capabilities.
2) The need to acquire credible deterrence designed primarily to prevent large-scale confrontation, which they

regard as beyond their capacity and therefore contrary to their interests. One specific dimension of their concept of deterrence was the ability, should basic deterrence fail, to take the war into arenas considered more advantageous to them so as to neutralize some of Israel's technological advantages.

3) The need to develop a strategy of attrition as a key to victory, given Israel's sensitivity to long wars and casualties. This perception was operationalized into the notion of "victory by avoiding defeat," which argues that the ability to survive a confrontation is the key to victory when the opponent fails to achieve a clear, unequivocal victory.

Based on these perceptions, a unique form of warfare evolved among these actors that emphasizes the following components:

1) Improving the survivability of the fighting force through sheltering and dispersion, reducing the electronic and visual "signature," and operating primarily in urban environments where they are surrounded by civilians and media.

2) Using mortars, rockets, and surface-to-surface missiles based on their simplicity, low cost, and potential to penetrate deep into Israel's territory (until recently), as well as the difficulty of tracing and attacking them (the large number of such tools available to these actors is conducive to survivability and extends their staying power).

3) Using weapon systems, operational modes, and other means that can produce high casualties among both civilians and military and focusing on abducting both civilians and military personnel, given Israel's high sensitivity in this matter.

4) Conducting media and public relations campaigns designed to deny domestic and international legitimacy to Israeli military actions and to undermine the Israeli public's staying power.

5) Confining combat to close-range engagements on the ground, in which, as they see it, many components of Israel's military technological superiority can be neutralized.

6) Acquiring the capability to contend with Israel's aerial superiority, given their understanding of the centrality of airpower in the IDF's current operational concept during and between wars.

One version of these developments was described a few years ago by Hassan Nasrallah, the leader of Hezbollah, in the following words: "This is a new and incomparable school of fighting, one that is placed between a regular army and guerrilla warfare."[1] Indeed, at issue is an impressive conceptual development, one that challenges the IDF's operational concept and requires a suitable intelligence and operational adaptation.

An entirely different dimension, one that will not be addressed fully here, regards unconventional weapons, with a particular emphasis on the nuclear area. Iraq began to develop military nuclear capability in the late 1970s, followed by Iran, Libya, and

Syria. Israel destroyed the Iraqi reactor and is reported to have destroyed a Syrian one as well. Libya voluntarily gave up its nuclear program, and Iran signed a deal to suspend development. At this point, the issue of nuclear strategy and deterrence declined in importance, but its shadow hovers over the region.

THE FIRST PALESTINIAN INTIFADA

The Palestinian Intifada and the First Gulf War, which took place at the same time, significantly challenged the IDF's original operational concept and left it initially without an appropriate response.

In a strict military sense, the intifada raised essential questions regarding the definition of a new phenomenon and its significance. The IDF was thrown into a confrontation with a civilian Palestinian population in which it lacked preparation or a conceptual framework enabling it to contend with the chain of events. One significant manifestation of this difficulty was the IDF's frequent use of excessive force. The intifada ended twenty years during which IDF deployment in the West Bank and Gaza was minimal: it required an increasing presence of military force and the establishment of new commands. The IDF was required to pursue missions that in other countries are defined as policing missions. More broadly, it shifted the IDF's attention away from the kind of warfare on which it had focused until that time. For the Israeli public and political system, the intifada demonstrated the limits of military power and the difficulties inherent in long-term occupation and control of a hostile population.

MILITARY OPERATIONS OF THE 1990S

The First Gulf War

Saddam Hussein's invasion of Kuwait in August 1990 led in January 1991 to the First Gulf War. Soon after the outbreak of that war, Saddam started to launch missiles at targets in Israel and Saudi Arabia, a tactic that he continued almost to the war's end.

On the eve of the First Gulf War, the Iraqis were broadly aware of the nature of the threat they were facing, but the structure of their military forces and traditional patterns of military thinking obstructed their ability to fully understand the significance of developments taking place in the West. Saddam's hopes that his forces would overcome the West's technological superiority during the ground campaign were dashed during the first hundred hours. Nevertheless, Saddam emerged from the war believing he could contend with the world's largest power and the coalition it had put together, though Iraq had been defeated in the Gulf War, lost a large part of its army, and had to abandon its unconventional capabilities. In the years following the war, Iraq was affected by harsh sanctions and had to contend with pervasive control and limitations on the employment of its military power. In the south and north of the country, no-fly zones were enforced by the US Air Force.

The First Gulf War is relevant to our discussion in three respects: First, it marks the beginning of a new era in the mode of employing the United States' military power, which clearly affected Israeli military thinking. Second, it demonstrated the threat of surface-to-surface missiles and marked the end of the era of "clean skies" that resulted from many years of Israeli Air Force superiority. The failure of the US Air Force to trace and neutralize Iraqi rocket launchers indicated the complexity of the professional challenges involved in dealing with mobile rocket launchers. It demonstrated a new direct threat to Israel from countries that do not share a border with it, which until that time could only participate in wars against Israel by dispatching forces and equipment to the confrontation states. It also demonstrated a greater capacity to hit Israel's home front and Israel's failure to possess or develop an adequate response to this capability. Third, it was the first war during which domestic and external limitations were imposed on Israel's use of military force in response to attack and provocation. These limitations derived partly from US diplomatic pressure but also from the Israeli leadership's perception that it did not possess an adequate response to the challenge. The war demonstrated that the original operational concept, which had been relevant to Israel's strategic environment during earlier decades, was no longer relevant due to changes in that environment.

In the war's aftermath, the Bush administration convened the Madrid Conference in an effort to take advantage of the new position and prestige enjoyed by the United States to resolve the Arab-Israeli conflict. The peace process launched in Madrid forced the Israeli political leadership to make tough choices regarding the fundamental question posed after the 1967 war: seek to hang on to the territories captured in the West Bank, the Gaza Strip, and the Golan Heights or continue to implement the concept of "territories for peace," which had been applied with Egypt and the Sinai in the search for a comprehensive solution to the Arab-Israeli conflict. In the Israeli elections of 1992, the camp supporting the territories for peace approach, headed by Yitzhak Rabin, won, and a three-year effort to come to terms with Syria and Palestinian nationalism followed. Rabin's tenure was marked by the first formulation of a new, not fully articulated, grand strategy. Rabin believed that the main threats to Israel were posed by Iraq and Iran in the eastern part of the region, and to deal with them he had to come to terms with Israel's immediate Arab neighbors. Rabin referred to his new policy as "changing Israel's order of priorities."[2] His policy led to the signing of the Oslo Accords with the PLO, the formation of the Palestinian Authority in Gaza and parts of the West Bank, and a second peace treaty with Jordan. Rabin (and his successors) failed to achieve a peace agreement with Syria. Rabin's Palestinian policy met with fierce opposition in Israel and ultimately led to his assassination. Rabin's partner, Shimon Peres, had a somewhat different grand strategy, or rather a grand vision, in that he believed that the key to managing Arab-Israeli relations was joint economic development of the region.

Rabin's "grand strategy" included cultivation of an intimate relationship with the United States, first with George H. W. Bush and then with Bill Clinton. Rabin mended the relationship that had been frayed by Yitzhak Shamir's Likud government, which had focused on keeping the West Bank and settling it. During the twenty years that followed his assassination, different prime ministers tended to choose either end of the spectrum in making similar choices. Peres, Barak, Olmert, and (surprisingly) Sharon maintained close coordination with the United States, while Netanyahu chose to confront both Clinton and Obama.

Public Discussion on Firepower

The public discussion of the IDF's operational concept that began in the 1980s continued into the 1990s, at which point it dealt specifically with the relationship between firepower and the ground maneuver. The commander of the Northern Command, General Yossi Peled, asked in a 1993 article "whether through precise fire in a static battle we can inflict on the enemy such heavy losses that it would bring the war to an end."[3] His conclusion was negative. He did not rule out the theoretical option of achieving victory in this manner but explained that it was incompatible with the unique conditions of Israel, a country devoid of strategic depth and under pressure to conclude wars swiftly. He concluded that there was no need to change the original operational concept, but it had to be adapted to the new circumstances, particularly to the threats presented to ground maneuver.

Public discussion of the IDF's operational concept ended during the 1990s, and in retrospect it seems that a decision was never reached within the IDF. At least through the decade's end, the IDF invested both in firepower and in improvements to its capacity to perform ground maneuver. But in practice

Israel's decision makers showed a clear preference for relying on firepower. This was manifested in the two military operations in Lebanon, Operation Accountability in 1993 and Operation Grapes of Wrath in 1996, when Israel used firepower rather than ground forces.

Accountability and Grapes of Wrath

These two military operations are, indeed, prominent milestones in the evolution of the IDF's distancing from its original operational concept toward preference for firepower. The argument has been made that the proximity of these operations to the First Gulf War is not accidental and that the preference for firepower derives from the lessons of that war. Israeli army officers did indeed observe that war and wrote about it, and it seems to have influenced the military thinking that underlay greater reliance on firepower. Nonetheless, such influence seems to have been marginal.

THE IDF AND ISRAELI SOCIETY

These changes can be traced to significant political and social developments in Israel. By the 1990s it was entirely clear that fundamental changes were taking place in the relationship between army and society in the country, and that the collectivist model of "a nation in uniform," which had been formed in the 1950s and remained effective into the 1980s, had been significantly diluted. This was chiefly manifested by the decline in immunity from public scrutiny and criticism that the IDF had enjoyed in earlier decades, as well as the diminished importance of military service as a manifestation of civic duty. These developments were well reflected in a speech delivered by the chief of staff, Major General Amnon Lipkin-Shahak, in a memorial for Prime Minister Yitzhak Rabin: "How far are we, my commander, from the days when the IDF uniform was a source of pride and a source of honor? . . . Evading military service is no longer a stain on the evader."[4]

A different manifestation of the change was the Supreme Court's intervention through a series of rulings considered precedential with regard to issues that had previously been regarded as entirely "military," which marked a loss of IDF autonomy in these matters. In this context, the Supreme Court forced the army to accept female candidates into flight training and blocked the advancement of a senior officer who had been found guilty of sexual harassment in disciplinary court. Rates of staying on beyond mandatory service declined, indicating that the IDF was no longer the attractive employer it had been in the past, and the ethos of adopting a military career declined in importance. The story of small start-up companies established by young gifted entrepreneurs coming out of military service in technological units and then sold to US corporations for enormous sums (Mirabilis and Chromatis, among others) became the model of success in globalized Israel of the 1990s. It affected the outlook of a large number of young soldiers, mostly from technological units, and forced the IDF to invest a huge effort to preserve the manpower of these units.

A number of researchers and the IDF itself identified these processes at the time and addressed their influence on such aspects as parents' involvement in the IDF, issues of loss and commemoration, the IDF's relationship with the media, women's service in the IDF, the staying power of civil society, and willingness to serve, particularly in reserve units. But what these observers failed to notice at that time was the impact of these developments on the IDF's ability to implement its original operational concept.

THE "LEBANESE MUD"

"Lebanese mud" was a term used in Israel in the 1980s and 1990s to refer to the high cost of keeping the IDF in South Lebanon. The sense of being stuck senselessly in Lebanon's "mud" was intensified over the 1990s and reached its zenith in 1997, after the "helicopters disaster" (seventy-three casualties) and the naval commandos disaster (twelve casualties). Shortly thereafter, the Four Mothers organization arose to oppose the IDF presence in Lebanon and contributed to the IDF's departure in May 2000.

From our perspective, the influence of the notion of "Lebanese mud" on the IDF is of particular interest. This notion, from the point of view of the mid-level officers who were engaged in either fighting or planning, is illustrated in the book published by Brigadier General Moshe (Chico) Tamir, which deals with the IDF's long sojourn in Lebanon. Tamir writes that "in the war in Lebanon, even though it was never stated explicitly, the understanding percolated gradually that nothing warranted losses."[5] According to Tamir, who also served as the Northern Command's chief of operations, a significant ground maneuver was almost inconceivable: "The prospect of the IDF entering Lebanon once again in order to defeat a terrorist organization was never seriously considered at any point after the withdrawal to the Security Zone in 1985."[6]

The activity in Lebanon during those years pinpointed questions concerning the legitimacy of military force. Indeed, the notion of legitimacy acquired increasing currency and became the cardinal consideration in discussions of military force in both the Lebanese and Palestinian arenas. The IDF's planners dealt with two different concepts: domestic legitimacy was used in discussions of consensus on military action in Israeli society, while international legitimacy was used in discussions of whether the international community would allow implementation of a particular military action. In retrospect, it seems that the frequent use of the term "legitimacy" enabled the IDF's leadership to deal implicitly rather than explicitly with the new social and political constraints in Israel. In any event, these constraints were in the background of discussions and decisions at the time.

TECHNOLOGICAL DEVELOPMENTS

By the 1990s, a series of technological developments fundamentally changed the mode of operating from the air. These broad technological developments had an influence on the Israeli Air Force. In the 1990s aircraft survivability and ability to penetrate deep into enemy territory had significantly improved due to developments in electronic warfare, stealth, unmanned drones, and the ability to launch weapons beyond the range of ground fire. At the same time, the air force acquired precision-guided munition that greatly enhanced its ability to inflict damage, as well as new systems of collecting information and exercising command and control.

In past decades, the IDF attitude toward technology was ambivalent. On the one hand there was a quest to acquire the most advanced equipment. The central role allocated to armored units and to the air force in the framework of the original operational concept reflected a belief that technological superiority could help overcome quantitative inferiority. But the Israeli officer corps, particularly in the ground forces, articulated great doubt over the years regarding technology's potential, as well as a concern that overreliance on technology could diminish the importance of the human dimension, which was traditionally seen as the IDF's most significant advantage.

This too seems to have changed in the 1990s. The maturity of the new technologies was accompanied by greater transparency, leading a large number of army officers to become aware of their availability. These officers began to rely increasingly on technological solutions in situations that in the past had required ordinary military power. Technology was gradually perceived as a way of reducing the risks of military power. This was manifested in the IDF's two major arenas during these years: Lebanon and Palestine.

AIR FORCE ACTIVITY IN LEBANON

Under these circumstances, the use of airpower became increasingly natural. With the exception of the two large-scale operations in 1993 and 1996, it was the helicopter units of the air force that were primarily engaged in the Lebanese arena until 1997. Fighter jets were used several dozen times every year, but in the years preceding the withdrawal (1998–2000), the air force was increasingly used in attack missions. The requirement of conducting "a perfect war" (without casualties and without environmental damage) in Lebanon led the senior political and military levels to assign a clear priority to aerial force in this arena. Thus, in 1998, fighter jets performed 231 offensive sorties in Lebanon; a year later the number rose to 669 sorties, and in the first five months of 2000, 602 offensive sorties were performed.

In the year that preceded the IDF's withdrawal from Lebanon, the Israeli Air Force conducted three offensive operations against Lebanon's economic and civilian infrastructure by way of exerting pressure on the Lebanese state to act against Hezbollah.

A DECADE OF DIPLOMACY AND
NEW PATTERNS OF CONFRONTATION

The quest for a comprehensive or partial settlement of the Arab-Israeli conflict, which had been launched with the Madrid Process and reached its zenith under Rabin and Peres in the mid-1990s, continued intermittently into 2011. The quest for settlement was largely facilitated by changes that had occurred in Israel's strategic environment, some of which are related to the consequences of the First Gulf War.

Rabin's assassination in November 1995 and Peres's loss to Benjamin Netanyahu in the parliamentary elections of May 1996 produced a hiatus in the peace process. Netanyahu promised to respect the Oslo Accords signed by his predecessors and signed the Wye River Memorandum in 1998, promising withdrawal from an additional 13 percent of the West Bank. Nonetheless, the Wye agreement was not implemented, and Netanyahu, while adhering to the letter of the Oslo Accords, emasculated them in practice. Netanyahu negotiated with Syria's president, Hafez al-Assad, through a mediator and conveyed his willingness to withdraw from the Golan in return for a peace settlement with Syria, but that mediation too led nowhere.

Between 1999 and 2011, several additional attempts were made by Israeli leaders who were willing to engage in far-reaching peace negotiations with either Syria or the Palestinians or both to achieve another major breakthrough in the peace process: Ehud Barak in 1999–2000 and Ehud Olmert in 2008. Both failed to achieve any agreement. As prime minister, Ariel Sharon underwent a profound transformation from the radical leader of the Israeli Right and patron of the settlement project into a leader willing to take bold actions to consolidate Israel's territorial scope. Sharon withdrew from the Gaza Strip and destroyed Israeli settlements in that area, and was ready to continue with a similar—though less ambitious—policy in the West Bank before his illness and incapacitation in 2006. Olmert was succeeded as prime minister by Netanyahu in

2009. Netanyahu paid lip service to the idea of the two-state solution with the Palestinians but failed to move forward in negotiating with their leadership. It is less well known that Netanyahu negotiated seriously with Syria's ruler, Bashar al-Assad, until the eve of the Syrian civil war in 2011. All told, the quest for a continuation of the Arab-Israeli peace process after Rabin's assassination was disappointing, so that Rabin's policy in the years 1992–95 was the only effective move in terms of a grand strategy to transform Israel's relationship with the Arab world.

In the course of the 1990s, a fundamental change in Israel's concept of the types of war it might be involved in took place. The original operational concept distinguished between current and fundamental security, and in fact focused on the ongoing threat of a confrontation with the regular armies of bordering states: Egypt, Syria, and Jordan. Changes in the strategic environment of the 1990s made clear that in addition to conventional war (now limited to a potential war with Syria), other types of confrontations were possible, which required a different pattern of thinking. One type was defined as limited confrontation with a nonstate actor, seen primarily as a confrontation with the Palestinians. The second was defined as confrontation with a state that did not share a border with Israel, such as Iraq and Iran. During the same years, it became apparent that the likelihood of confrontation with Syria was smaller, so that resources should be allocated to a buildup of power designed to achieve decisive victory in the other types of confrontation.

These new types of confrontation were seen as challenging the IDF's original operational concept and the notion of decisive victory achieved through ground maneuver. Limited confrontation required domestic and international legitimacy that could hardly be obtained for ground maneuver. Confrontation with a state that did not share a border with Israel was seen as a bigger challenge to the original concept given the impossibility of employing ground forces. Israel's military thinkers were challenged to produce a new conceptual framework that would deal with how to achieve a decisive victory and implement war aims when ground forces were not an option.

THE US PERSPECTIVE

While this section of the monograph focuses on the IDF's operational concept, it is important to emphasize that the increasing preference assigned to firepower was not a distinctive Israeli phenomenon. A similar (and clearly influential) trend could be discerned in the United States in the aftermath of the First Gulf War. This was apparent in a series of confrontations: the punitive campaigns in Iraq (1996 and 1998), the offensive raids in Sudan and Afghanistan in 1998 in response to attacks on US embassies, and the confrontation with the Serbs in Bosnia (1995) and Kosovo (1999).

Of these confrontations, the Kosovo one is the most interesting. It was seen by many, in Israel and elsewhere, as the first example of a confrontation decided purely by airpower. The US perspective was more sober, linking the employment of force in this engagement with the social and political constraints that shaped its distinctive context. Thus, when the NATO commander, General Wesley Clark, described the Kosovo campaign, he referred to distinctive features such as "the exclusive reliance on airpower, fear of civilian losses on both sides, the debate on transition to a ground campaign" and explained that "they were affected by deeper factors."[7] The factors he mentioned are the same social and political constraints analyzed above.

3

FACING REALITY:
LEBANON AND GAZA

I srael's Second Lebanon War in 2006 brought to a head the
issue of the IDF's "new" operational concept, but before
dealing with that significant event, it is important to examine
two important landmarks in the evolution that culminated in
that war: the withdrawal from Lebanon in May 2000 and the
outbreak of the Second Intifada in September of that year.

THE WITHDRAWAL FROM LEBANON

The IDF's original operation concept placed particular emphasis on shifting the war to enemy territory and occupying such
territory. In this context, the IDF's withdrawal from Lebanon
represented a significant milestone in deviating from this concept. At issue was not the simple evacuation of the territory; the
IDF had withdrawn in the past from occupied territories after
the Sinai war and after the October War, and in accordance
with the peace treaty with Egypt and the Oslo Accords. Still,

the circumstances under which the unilateral withdrawal from Lebanon took place reflected, in the view of many, the pointlessness of holding on to territory beyond Israel's borders. From this point it was a short step to discussing the logic of occupying territory in an age in which holding on to such territory is no longer an asset. The unilateral withdrawal from Gaza in August 2005 added a particular edge to this question.

The withdrawal from Lebanon in 2000 ended eighteen years of Israeli presence there and was supposed to put an end also to the "Lebanese mud." But the abduction and killing of three IDF soldiers on the foothills of Mount Hermon on October 7, 2000, five months after the withdrawal, accelerated progress toward the Second Lebanon War. Israel left Lebanon determined not to return and was in fact reluctant to respond to the abduction of the soldiers. Prime Minister Ehud Barak believed at the time that Israel should exercise traditional deterrence from the Israeli side of the international border with regard to Lebanon. The abduction of the three soldiers was a challenge to that deterrence, but both the political and military levels were determined not to return to the "Lebanese mud." This message was internalized, and mounting significant ground maneuver in Lebanon was seen as less and less relevant. An operational plan named Defender of the Country had been completed, but it included several levels of operation that should have guaranteed that ground maneuver would be used only when all other options had been exhausted.

In parallel, Israel adopted a strategic military concept of "containment" centered around the idea of the Syrian leverage, based on the view that Syria was responsible for developments in Lebanon and that aerial force could be employed against Syria with greater efficacy. The assumption was that using aerial force against Syria could force the Syrians to exercise their influence over Hezbollah and restrain the organization. This plan was implemented on several occasions after the withdrawal from Lebanon. Thus, in April and July 2001, Syrian radar systems in Lebanon were attacked to signal to Damascus the need to restrain Hezbollah. But the most distinctive manifestation of this concept was a GHQ exercise called Fire Stones 9, in which no ground forces were employed.

Israelis perceived the departure of Syrian military forces from Lebanon in April 2005 as undermining the foundations of the "Syrian leverage" concept and requiring a more direct approach to exercising force against Hezbollah. This perception underlay the preparation of a new operational plan for dealing directly with Hezbollah (Highland Waters) through ground maneuver. The plan had not been completed prior to the outbreak of the Second Lebanon War in July 2006. In parallel, a second operational program (Icebreaker) was developed that reflected the preference to avoid ground maneuver. The purpose of that plan was to create a new and different situation in the Lebanese arena in case of overall escalation or an exceptional event, through large-scale exercise of firepower without a large-scale ground operation. The failure to complete the Highland Waters plan and the partial development of Icebreaker reflect the confusion that prevailed at the time at IDF headquarters over ground maneuver in Lebanon.

COPING WITH THE SECOND INTIFADA
(OPERATION EBB AND FLOW)

After the signing of the Oslo Accords, Israeli politicians assumed that the historic conflict with the Palestinians could be resolved through negotiations, in the course of which both parties would be required to make massive concessions. The Israeli leadership was fully aware of the depth of the controversy with the Palestinians over major issues, and they assumed that by 2000 an outbreak of violence was likely. Yet most of Israel's decision makers believed that ultimately the Palestinian strategy was to reach a solution through negotiations. From that perspective, the Israelis assumed that even though violent eruptions had to be anticipated, they would be focused and brief and would end at the negotiating table. Israeli leadership did not estimate that it would have to face a massive terrorist campaign predicated on a Palestinian attempt to hit Israel's population centers and test its stamina.

This view led Israel's decision makers in the immediate aftermath of the outbreak of violence in late September 2000 to assume that Yasser Arafat aimed to induce Israel to make further concessions on the main contested issues (Jerusalem and the Palestinian refugees), beyond the concessions offered by Ehud Barak at the Camp David summit in July 2000. The Israeli evaluation was that Arafat had resorted to violence to set in motion three efforts:

1) to break the willpower of Israeli society, which in his view had limited staying power;

2) to mobilize the Arab world to support his positions;
3) to bring about greater international involvement.

These efforts, he estimated, would finally lead to a resolution of the conflict according to his original points of departure.

During the early phase of the Second Intifada, Israel sustained about one hundred casualties (most of them in shootings and by roadside bombs), but the negotiations continued, with two summits taking place between senior Israeli and Palestinian negotiators in mid-October 2000 and early January 2001, and some of the coordination mechanisms established after the formation of the Palestinian Authority were preserved. The operational guidelines given to the IDF during the confrontation's early months derived from an assumption that the confrontation could be contained and that the Palestinian Authority would return as swiftly as possible to the negotiating table. The IDF was instructed "to contain" the unfolding chain of events. The instructions specifically referred to the need to prevent regional deterioration and international involvement in the conflict and led the IDF to implement a policy of defensive activity and focused response.

Although the Palestinian terrorist wave, much of it mounted by Hamas, was not checked during the first months of the confrontation, Israel continued to see the Palestinian Authority and the mechanism it controlled as the principal actors that could—and had to—act to terminate it. Israel's decision makers felt that insufficient pressure had been exerted on the Palestinian Authority, and the IDF was therefore ordered to increase the pressure. This instruction was translated into an operational scheme aimed at creating continuous pressure on the Palestinian Authority in order to induce it to fight terrorism. It was implemented by using the air force to attack the Palestinian Authority's infrastructure as well as authorizing the IDF to operate in area A (under full Palestinian control since the signing of Oslo II in September 1995). IDF activity in area A was limited by the need to take into account international diplomatic opinion, but the September 11, 2001, terrorist attacks on the United States transformed US and international outlooks on terrorism and greatly expanded Israel's freedom of action. Several months earlier, in February 2001, Ehud Barak had lost the special elections for the post of prime minister, and Ariel Sharon formed a new government and in time adopted his own strategy for fighting the intifada.

Israel's more aggressive line was manifested in the final weeks of 2001. During this period, the Palestinians increased their pressure through suicide bombings, which led the Israeli government to announce on December 3 that the Palestinian Authority was an entity supporting terrorism. Israeli Air Force planes and helicopters attacked Palestinian governmental centers, including Arafat's own bureau, and the IDF destroyed the Dahaniya airport in the Gaza Strip. The siege of the Palestinian cities of Nablus and Ramallah was tightened, and IDF forces entered A areas around these cities. Yet another suicide bombing led the government to announce that Arafat was "irrelevant," to stop all communications with him, and to intensify IDF activity: IDF forces took over several neighborhoods in Ramallah, positioned tanks in front of Arafat's office, and limited his movements.

But this massive offensive did not put an end to the suicide attacks. Their number and intensity increased. A series of Palestinian suicide attacks between August 2001 and March 2002 resulted in the death of hundreds of Israelis. During March 2002 alone, 136 Israelis were killed. This produced a broad consensus in Israel that a large-scale operation was warranted, and to implement it a concept of ground maneuver was required that would take into account the difficulties of operating in a dense urban area and cope with the anticipated repercussions in Israel and abroad. Operation Defensive Shield in April 2002 was carried out in line with a concept developed by field commanders at the brigade and division level. This concept had been tried in a series of smaller-scale operations during the preceding months and proved successful in coping with the operational and political challenges that had constrained Israel's activity during the previous year.

Over the following year, Israel relied less and less on aerial power. As the Palestinian Authority's apparatus eroded, the number of relevant targets declined while Israel's control of the terrain opened new venues of activity. Most of Israel's aerial activity took the form of targeted killings of Hamas activists. The Israeli Air Force was primarily engaged in preparations for potential involvement once the US invasion of Iraq was launched (at the end of March 2003). The IDF's activities in the Palestinian cities significantly diminished Palestinian ability to launch terrorist activities, but suicide bombings continued to inflict significant casualties during the following months. Hamas was responsible for a large part of these attacks, and in mid-2003 Israel began a focused campaign against the movement and its leaders. The first major operation in this context was the attempt to kill Abdel Aziz Rantisi on June 2003. The attempt failed, but Hamas agreed to a ceasefire (*hudna*) that began on June 29 and ended in late August of that year. Between June 10, 2003, and April 17, 2004, twenty-six targeted killing operations were directed mostly against Hamas and Palestinian Islamic jihad activists, both senior and junior. This campaign reached its peak in March–April 2004, when Hamas's leaders, Sheikh Ahmad Yassin and Abdel Aziz Rantisi, were killed.

These operations were supplemented by construction of the Separation Wall along much of the Green Line between Israel and the West Bank. The construction of this wall generated both international criticism and political opposition inside Israel by those who viewed its construction as a reaffirmation of the relevance of the Green Line.

By the end of 2004, it was clear that Israel had succeeded in defeating the Second Intifada. The years 2001–04 saw one of the most difficult crises in Israel's history, but Israeli society proved that it had the resilience Arafat had thought it lacked. Ariel Sharon, who led the campaign and was credited with the victory, came to enjoy a position of unprecedented power and prestige in Israeli politics that enabled him to take bold decisions in 2005.

A NEW OPERATIONAL CONCEPT

In the final years of the twentieth century and the early years of the twenty-first century, the Israeli leadership, civilian as well as military, fully aware of the need to rethink the IDF's military strategy, engaged in several efforts to reformulate the country's national security policy and the IDF's military plan. One major effort was conducted by the Meridor Commission. Dan Meridor, chairman of the Knesset's Foreign and Defense Affairs Committee, headed a commission that invested a major effort in reformulating Israel's national security plan. The committee's work lasted from 2004 to 2006, and its report was submitted to Prime Minister Olmert. The commission's main recommendation was to add a fourth-dimension defense to the three pillars of Israel's traditional strategy (general deterrence, early warning, and decisive victory). The commission's report had a limited practical impact on the policies of either the government or the IDF, but Israel has put a big effort into developing a multilayered antimissile defense and some effort into preparing the home front for missile and rocket attacks.

Another effort was conducted during the same period at the initiative of chief of staff Dan Halutz. This effort was preceded by an interview given to the IDF's armored corps publication in October 1999 by General Shlomo Yanai, head of the IDF's planning division. In it, Yanai presented the broad lines for the IDF multiyear plan. Yanai explained the change in types of confrontations anticipated and how this change affects preferences for the buildup of forces. When asked about the changes, he started by describing the effort to formulate a new operational concept for the IDF. Yanai explained that "formulating an operational concept is a necessary stage in building a focused force particularly in an age of shortage of resources. Therefore, we began by putting together a concept for operating force—

updated for future challenges." One of the principles described by Yanai referred to the relationship between ground maneuver and firepower, at which point he argued that "at the end of the day, decisive victory is achieved by 'planting a flag.'"[1]

In the years following that interview, numerous discussions were held in the IDF regarding a "new" operational concept. These discussions took place against the backdrop of budget cuts, but they also reflected ripeness for a fundamental discussion of the original operational concept, given ongoing criticism of that concept and the sense that it was no longer relevant to contemporary challenges. This discussion was summed up in a document regarding the IDF's operational concept that was distributed in April 2006 under the signature of the chief of staff, Dan Halutz.

The importance of the document does not lie in its impact on decision making during the Second Lebanon War. In the aftermath of the war, the Winograd Commission was convened to investigate the conduct of the war. In its report, the commission noted that the document itself had little impact on the exercise of force during the war and on the deficiencies that were manifested. The document had been published in April 2006, and it is doubtful whether it had been seriously studied by its readers in the short time that separated its publication from the outbreak of the war. Its importance in our context lies in the manner in which the IDF leadership interpreted the impact of the developments described above on the IDF's operational concept.

One of the main conclusions of the Halutz paper was that changes in the strategic environment gave a new significance to the territorial component. According to the paper, changes in the

strategic environment created a limitation concerning the legitimacy of occupying territory and holding it as a bargaining chip.
The new concept also held that holding territory with a large
force plays into the enemy's hands and could lead to a guerilla
war and the need to manage the civilian population. These statements undoubtedly reflect the influence of the social and political constraints mentioned above on military thinking, as well as
fundamental changes in—and deviation from—the original
operational concept. Underlying the new concept was, to a great
extent, the notion of changing the role of firepower from an
auxiliary component to a cardinal component in achieving decisive victory. The document did not argue that wars can be
decided by aerial force alone, nor did it abandon ground maneuver, but it did reflect a change in the relationship between the
roles of ground maneuver and firepower. A closer reading of the
text also indicates that the new concept included a different view
of ground maneuver. It now envisaged ground maneuver based
on lighter forces directly aimed at the enemy's power centers.

The IDF's traditional concept of ground maneuver conducted by a large order of battle was now, according to the
Halutz document, seen as less and less relevant due to both the
emphasis it placed on occupying territory and the perception
that this approach would exact high casualties. Under these
circumstances, it was necessary to develop a new concept of
ground maneuver that could deal with the new constraints.
Such a concept had been developed for the West Bank operational arena, and it had facilitated the employment of Israel's
military power in Operation Defensive Shield and subsequent
operations. But in fact it was the exception rather than the rule.

The continued construction of Israel's order of battle along traditional lines and the emphasis given to the absorption of the Merkava tanks reflected the persistence of the old kind of ground maneuver.

Additional efforts to develop an alternative concept of ground maneuver were not completed, with the net result that on July 12, when the Second Lebanon War broke out, the IDF did not possess a concept of ground maneuver that was relevant to the challenge presented by Hezbollah. The only concept available to the IDF was the traditional concept as reshaped by the October War of 1973. This concept could possibly have proved effective during the Lebanon War. It is also possible that domestic and international legitimacy would have emerged to facilitate its application, but the IDF that conducted the Second Lebanon War had been affected by years of neglect. This neglect was the result of new technologies, the application of lessons drawn—correctly or incorrectly—from recent US experience, budget cuts, and the IDF's preoccupation during the previous years with the Palestinian terrorist challenge.

MASSIVE CHANGES IN THE TWENTY-FIRST CENTURY

Israel's Second Lebanon War in 2006 brought the new challenges to Israel's national security into evidence, exposed Israel's failure to conceptualize and implement adequate responses to them, and forced Israel's political and military system to come up with at least a partial response to these challenges.

But the new strategy of "the other side" provided just part of the backdrop to the Second Lebanon War. Its significance should be evaluated in the context of the massive changes that had taken place in the Middle East in the early years of the new century, thereby transforming Israel's regional strategic environment:

1) The Bush administration's decision to invade Iraq in 2003 and to topple Saddam Hussein and his regime had far-reaching consequences for the whole region. The United States established a massive military presence in the region. In the aftermath of a striking initial military victory, the United States found itself bogged down for years in a country it had to rule and administer, fighting a Sunni insurgency and al-Qaeda terrorism. George Bush's boldness had contradictory effects: it generated opposition and hatred but also served to moderate the conduct of countries like Libya and Iran. Libya was persuaded to give up its nuclear program, while Iran became interested in opening a dialogue with the United States and modifying, though not canceling, its nuclear program. The removal of Saddam Hussein, who had served as a bulwark against the projection of Iranian influence into the core area of the Middle East, enabled Tehran to expand its presence and influence in Lebanon and Syria. The Bush administration justified its invasion of Iraq by arguing that it led to the expansion of democracy in the Arab world. This did not quite happen, but in two instances—the

Cedar Revolution in Lebanon in 2005 and the Palestinian elections of January 2006—Washington was supportive of what could be described as successful instances of democratization. Washington extended considerable support to Prime Minister Fouad Siniora of Lebanon and exerted massive pressure on Ariel Sharon to allow the elections of January 2006 in the Palestinian Authority, which ended with a victory of Hamas over Fatah and eventually to Hamas's takeover of the Gaza Strip.

2) In Turkey, Recep Tayyip Erdoğan, after achieving a plurality (though not a majority) in the parliamentary elections of 2003, became prime minister. Erdoğan, an Islamist who drew the right lessons from the failure of Necmettin Erbakan's earlier effort to apply his Islamism to Turkish politics, proceeded gradually. Erdoğan was able to weaken the older secular elites, primarily the military, and in time became a powerful authoritarian ruler. Erdoğan's Islamism combined with Turkey's rejection by the European Union to focus his attention on the Middle East and on other neighboring areas that had earlier belonged to the Ottoman Empire. A policy sometimes called "Neo-Ottomanism" brought Turkey back to the Middle East as a full, powerful participant. As an Islamist, Erdoğan supports the Muslim Brotherhood and, in the Palestinian context, Hamas and its rule in Gaza. Erdoğan led a policy of distancing Turkey from its close strategic partnership with Israel, positioning his government as a bitter critic of Israel and its Palestinian policy.

3) As mentioned above, Saddam's removal opened the gateway for greater Iranian influence in the core area of the Middle East, particularly in Lebanon but also in Gaza. Tehran took advantage of Mubarak's fall in Egypt in 2011 to send navy units through the Suez Canal to the Mediterranean. The combined effect of Turkey's re-entry into the Middle East after decades of Ataturk's European orientation and Iran's reinforced activism in the region was dramatic. Two large, powerful Muslim non-Arab regional powers led by Islamist governments fully joined the Middle Eastern system. From Israel's point of view, these were both negative developments, adding two bitter and powerful enemies to its strategic map.

4) Iran began its nuclear program in the aftermath of the Iran-Iraq War, undoubtedly seeking to obtain a nuclear arsenal. In 2003, reacting to the US invasion of Iraq, it modified its plan and agreed to enter into a dialogue with the United States and a negotiation with the European powers. It continued to push ahead with several components of its nuclear program but was careful not to be seen as pursuing a nuclear weapon. The process of negotiation over its nuclear program proceeded slowly, but the shadow of Iranian nuclear potential was cast over the region.

5) In Russia, Vladimir Putin, who had come to power in 2000, was busy building his personal power and pursuing a policy of rebuilding Russia's international position after years of humiliation. Putin took advantage

of the high cost of oil to rebuild Russia's military capacity and diplomatic influence, which would be fully manifested in the Middle East in the coming years.

THE SECOND LEBANON WAR

The Second Lebanon War is the name that Israel's government retroactively gave to the military confrontation with Hezbollah that took place between July 12 and August 14, 2006. The war was part of the ongoing conflict between Israel and Hezbollah that began with the organization's founding in 1982. It was triggered by a Hezbollah attack on an IDF patrol on the Lebanese Israeli border that led to the killing of five Israeli soldiers and the abduction of two of their bodies. The war ended when the parties agreed to accept Security Council Resolution 1701, which called for a ceasefire and reinforcement of the United Nations peacekeeping force in South Lebanon. Israel also conducted a simultaneous large-scale military operation against Hamas and other organizations in the Gaza Strip following the abduction (on June 25) of an IDF soldier near the fence separating Israel from the Gaza Strip.

The Second Lebanon War was a seminal event, an important milestone in the gradual transition away from the IDF's original operational concept. The war exposed the full significance of the new challenges and threats presented to Israel by the emergence on two of its borders of semi-sovereign nonstate actors combining several forms of warfare, equipped with rockets and missiles, and in Hezbollah's case, supported by Iran and Syria. The war thus confronted the IDF with Hezbollah, by now a familiar adversary, a distinctive representative of "a new generation of enemies" that had developed in previous decades: an organization possessing significant military capacity and a semi-military structure, operating in patterns and straddling the lines separating a regular army from a guerrilla force. Strategically, given the circumstances, Israeli decision makers made a conscious choice to launch a "deterrent operation," which was, in their eyes, distinctly different from "an operation seeking decisive victory." Still, the conceptual infrastructure for the conduct of such an operation had yet to crystallize, and the manner in which different levels had to implement it exposed discrepancies that led to the use of problematic rhetoric as well as several wrong decisions. In operative terms, this encounter led Israel to a mode of operation that was severely criticized. The military preferred to rely almost exclusively on the firepower of the air force and artillery, and was hesitant to use its ground forces in ground maneuver. A significant ground maneuver, as distinct from limited raids, was not carried out until late in the war, and then it was implemented partially and terminated before accomplishing its goals.

In retrospect, deterrence had been accomplished. Since the war, Israel has enjoyed ten years of unusual calm on its northern border that derives at least in part to this war and its outcome. And yet, the war remained in public memory as a missed opportunity, not necessarily because of the large number of Israeli casualties (120 soldiers and 42 civilians) but rather because of the large gap between the expectations generated at the war's onset and the manner in which it was concluded. The IDF, with all its advanced capacities, could not put an end to the ongoing rocket attacks in the north of Israel, and at the war's end, thirty-four days later, Hezbollah had not been defeated. The four thousand rockets that landed in Israel's territory left many Israelis with difficult questions regarding the country's military might and the IDF's ability to deal with current challenges. Such questions continued to occupy the Israeli public through additional campaigns over the past decade in the Gaza Strip (Cast Lead at the end of 2008, Pillar of Defense in 2010, and Protective Edge in 2014).

We will now deal with the strategic and operational aspects of Israel's employment of military power during the Second Lebanon War, focusing on the discrepancies between the sense of a missed opportunity and the actual outcome as seen from a ten-year perspective. Our main argument is that the Second Lebanon War was first and foremost a powerful expression of a new kind of war confronted by Israel. Some broad characteristics of this brand of war had been familiar to Israelis for more than two decades, but their consolidation into a single intense confrontation challenged the political leadership, the senior military command, the IDF fighters, and the broad public to adapt their patterns of thought and action to a novel situation. The postwar criticism of the war's conduct at all levels was also affected by this difficulty despite correctly identifying flaws and failures.

WAS IT A WAR?

On July 12, 2012, on the sixth anniversary of the outbreak of the Second Lebanon War, Ehud Olmert, who had served as prime minister during the war, delivered a lecture at a conference held by the Institute for National Security Studies (INSS) at Tel Aviv University. He opened his lecture with a general comment that "it would be an exaggeration to refer to the military effort invested by Israel in Lebanon in the summer of 2006 as a war."[2] During the war itself, the government headed by Olmert refrained from using the term "war." An appeal to the Supreme Court of Justice to instruct the government to exercise its authority and declare war was rejected at the time, and the court explicitly stated that in its view, the events at hand did not constitute a war. The senior military level also refrained from defining the events as a war.

This was not accidental. For most people, including civilian and military decision makers, the image and concept of a war were shaped by the patterns that had characterized wars in the modern era since the middle of the eighteenth century. "Modern war" as defined as Carl von Clausewitz (among others) was total in its intensity and industrial in its essence; it was conducted between states with a distinctly political goal in mind and ended as a rule in a clear-cut fashion. These characteristics were supplemented by the concept of a military "decisive victory," identified with occupying the enemy's territory and destroying its forces. Israel's wars in 1956 ("a hundred hours to the Suez Canal") and in 1967 ("six days in June") helped shape an image of the short decisive war that even the October War of 1973 failed to crack.

This was the image that shaped the consciousness of many Israelis in the summer of 2006 and made it difficult for them to recognize that at issue was a war, though a new brand of war. Indeed, so powerful was the image that the quest for a swift, clear-cut decision in a short war underlay scrutiny of the war's course and outcome. But the 2006 war, as well as subsequent military operations, demonstrate that reality had changed. The Second Lebanon War was not a modern war according to the characteristics that had been common since the Napoleonic wars. It was not conducted between two nation-states, it was not total, and the two parties did not seek decisions through occupying territories or destroying forces. The war and the three subsequent operations in Gaza put in question the realism of the quest to shorten the war and achieve a clear and unequivocal decision.

WHAT DID ISRAEL TRY TO ACCOMPLISH?

It is commonly accepted that the war exposed serious flaws regarding decision making on the strategic level in Israel. It is clear today that even though the threat of abduction was concrete (it had been attempted by Hezbollah in November 2005), the political and military Israeli leadership lacked a comprehensive, coherent concept as to how to contend with such a challenge and its larger ramifications.

This state of affairs derived from several sources, some of which were the product of far-reaching changes in Israel's political and military leadership. In January 2006, Ehud Olmert replaced Ariel Sharon, who was in a coma, as prime minister and was subsequently elected to that post. In May 2006, about a month prior to the war, Olmert appointed as minister of defense Amir Peretz, who had previously dealt primarily with social and economic issues. It was an exceptional moment in Israel's history that both the prime minister and the minister of defense lacked significant defense or military experience. The IDF leadership had also undergone far-reaching changes in the year preceding the war. The chief of staff was Dan Halutz, the first air force officer to be appointed to this post. He started his tenure in May 2005, after serving about a year as deputy chief of staff, and his main challenge during his first year in office was the IDF's withdrawal from the Gaza Strip, which was implemented successfully. Halutz's GHQ was not essentially different from earlier ones. It was mostly composed of ground forces generals with two exceptions: the director of military intelligence, General Amos Yadlin, who was appointed by Halutz in January 2006, and the commander of the air force, General Eliezer Shkedi, who replaced Halutz in April 2004.

It is difficult to identify Israel's goals in the Second Lebanon War, since the information that has been released clearly indicates that Israel entered the war without conducting a fundamental discussion of the war's political aims. During the first discussion held by the government, it was not clear to most ministers that Israel was actually in the first phase of a war, and many of them referred to the military activity as a responsive act focused in time and scope. Most ministers were of the opinion that the abduction required a sharp response, but no serious discussion was held of the broader significance of the Israeli action and its general aims. At the end of the meeting, a government statement was published that cast responsibility on the government of Lebanon but singled out Hezbollah as responsible for the abduction and designated to pay the price for it. The statement warned of a possible significant attack on the home front and announced that a small team of cabinet members was being formed to approve specific military operations. This team did indeed meet several times to approve targets but not to conduct a broader discussion of the larger goals of the military operation and the relationship between such goals and specific targets.

The clearest formulation of the war's political aims can be found in a speech delivered by Prime Minister Olmert in the Knesset on July 17, 2006, five days after the war's start. In this speech Olmert presented highly ambitious goals for the war that included, among other things, the return of the abducted soldiers, Hezbollah's ouster from South Lebanon, and the deployment in the region of the Lebanese army according to Security Council Resolution 1559. In the war's aftermath, Olmert formed a commission of inquiry to investigate the conduct of the war (the Winograd Commission). In his testimony before the commission, as well as in a lecture he gave in 2012, Olmert played down the importance of the July 17 speech and argued that the statements he had made were designed to serve as a deterrent as well as to raise the morale of the Israeli public and the fighting force.

In many respects, the clearest articulation of the war's concrete aims was provided by the IDF when it presented to the government, on the first day of fighting, its interpretation of the war's political aims. From the IDF's presentation, it emerges that its leadership understood that the military operation's strategic purpose was first and foremost to restore and deepen Israeli deterrence. This was to be achieved by demonstrating Israeli willingness to exact a disproportionately high price for hostile activity against it despite the clear threat to the home front. Also evident in the IDF's presentation was an emphasis on the responsibility of the government of Lebanon for the security situation in the south of the country. This presentation reflected the army's understanding that the military action as such could not bring about the return of the abducted soldiers. What the IDF had in mind was the creation of conditions that would facilitate negotiations for their return.

A scrutiny of the materials that have been published on discussions conducted early in the war indicates that Israel wanted primarily to restore its deterrent image, which had been seriously cracked due to the combined effect of two abductions that took place in arenas from which Israel had withdrawn unilaterally. Israeli decision makers felt that under these circumstances, it was necessary to respond sharply. The statements made that day dealt more with the scope and intensity of the Israeli response and less with the positive political goals that military actions should accomplish. In fact, the government of Israel decided not to go to war but rather to launch a military action that would send a clear message and prevent future abductions.

WHAT TASKS WERE ASSIGNED TO THE IDF?

In the evening discussions held by the cabinet on the first days of fighting, there were three approaches to the question of the objects of Israel's actions: one argued that the force should be directed at the Lebanese state, the second argued it should be directed at Syria, and the third that it should directed against Hezbollah.

The chief of staff, Major General Dan Halutz, saw Israel's response to the abduction as a turning point in its view of the problem posed by Hezbollah and Lebanese government responsibility in this matter. He proposed to the political level the strategic idea that had crystallized among the General Staff during the day: creating heavy pressure on the government of Lebanon to exercise its authority and deal with Hezbollah. This was to be achieved by inflicting serious damage to Lebanon's national infrastructure, primarily the power and transportation systems. The chief of staff was of course aware of the Lebanese government's weakness, and it seems that underlying this proposal was an assessment that such attacks would lead the international community to intervene and take the side of the Lebanese government. Another aspect of the same idea was the belief that the damages would make the Lebanese population recognize that actions taken by Hezbollah, which had presented itself as "the defender of Lebanon," actually brought massive destruction to the country. Specifically, the army suggested that two power stations be attacked so as to destroy 20–30 percent of Lebanon's electric power. In addition, it suggested attacking additional Hezbollah targets, including its broadcasting station.

The political level rejected the chief of staff's ideas, as well as another idea presented by the head of the Mossad, who suggested that targets in Syria also be attacked. The political level rejected both ideas and opted for hitting Hezbollah directly. The decision was influenced, among other things, by a message transmitted to the government by the United States that emphasized the importance of preserving Fouad Siniora's government in Lebanon. The Bush administration was very supportive of the Siniora government, which it saw as a manifestation of change in Lebanon and a major success in Washington's campaign for democratization and reform in Lebanon.

The political level authorized the IDF to put in practice an operational program prepared by the air force during the previous several years, which included a preemptive attack on Hezbollah rockets. This was a bold and risky concept since most rockets had been hidden in civilian homes, mostly on the fringes of villages. The army hesitated to recommend this plan due to the fear of large-scale civilian casualties. In the event, the number of casualties was much smaller, but the political leadership's willingness to authorize this operation reflected its perception of the intensity of response required by circumstances.

The IDF's interpretation of the specific tasks assigned to it appears in the operational command published on that day. From its formulation, it is clear that the IDF was instructed to destroy Hezbollah's rocket launchers; to diminish the organization's launching capacity; to target its personnel, commands, and infrastructure, "symbols and assets," as well as to destroy Hezbollah's infrastructure close to the Israeli border in order to create a special security space in that region. At the same time, the IDF was instructed to impose an aerial and naval blockade to prevent the supply of weapons to Hezbollah from Syria and Iran.

A significant ground operation was not seriously discussed on the first day. When it was, during the next few days, most decision makers on both the political and senior military levels were opposed to the idea.

It is an interesting point that the guidelines given to the IDF did not specifically address the need to bring a swift end to the launching of short-range rockets. Both levels minimized the importance of the short-range rockets and thus missed to a large extent their central position in Hezbollah's thinking. Israel's decision makers understood that Israel's home front would be hit by rockets—a fact that was emphasized in internal discussions and public statements—but it seems that the decision makers underestimated the importance of this issue. This was reinforced by the perception that Israel had no adequate response to the problem of the rockets. A ground move was not seen as likely to end these attacks.

HOW WAS MILITARY FORCE EMPLOYED?

First Phase

During the war's first phase, the IDF acted primarily to neutralize Hezbollah's strategic capabilities and to signal to the organization that a fundamental change had taken place in

Israel's policy. This phase lasted for about a week, from the beginning of the war to July 19. During this phase, Israel was hit by 625 rockets (an average of one hundred rockets a day), and thirteen civilians and fourteen soldiers were killed (including the soldiers killed on the first day). The rockets hit, among other sites, the cities of Haifa and Tiberias. During this phase, Israel's military action enjoyed broad support among Israelis and the international public.

This phase mostly involved the air force, which acted primarily against Hezbollah's medium- and long-range rockets. In addition, Hezbollah's symbols of sovereignty in Lebanon (the Dahiya quarter in Beirut and Hezbollah's installation in Baalbek), bridges, and lines of communications and command were attacked. In parallel, an aerial and naval blockade of Lebanon was put in place to interdict supplies from Syria and Iran. The air force also attacked convoys moving military equipment from Syria to Lebanon. During this phase, ground forces were employed only to destroy Hezbollah's positions along the fence separating Lebanon from Israel.

Second Phase

In retrospect, it is clear that Israel's mode of operation had run its course at the end of the first week. The intelligence that guided the raids against Hezbollah's rockets and additional installations had been fully used. Operational plans that the IDF had prepared before the war had identified this issue in time and determined that at this point it should suspend the raids, examine their impact, and if need be, launch a significant ground operation. However, decision makers did not seriously consider implementing this plan. Still, the sense that the aerial effort had failed to inflict sufficient damage on Hezbollah and the continuation of rocket attacks brought on a transition to the war's second phase. This phase, which lasted from July 19 to July 31, included a sustained effort to hit rockets from the air and a limited ground maneuver that was designed not to conquer territory or to directly destroy short-term rockets, but to hit Hezbollah activists. It took the form of limited raids on spaces controlled by Hezbollah. In this context, such raids were conducted on the villages of Bint Jbeil and Maroun a-Ras, and later in other areas.

One of the main characteristics of this phase was a significant decline in international support for the Israeli operation, which reached a low point at the end of July in the aftermath of an incident during which several Lebanese citizens were killed or injured inside a home that collapsed after an air raid in the village of Kana. During this phase of the war, about 1,250 rockets (a daily average of about a hundred) hit Israeli territory, and seven civilians and twenty-one soldiers were killed.

Third Phase

A cabinet discussion, held on July 31, led to giving approval to the IDF to extend the ground operation in Lebanon and to create a special security zone six kilometers wide. This discussion marked the beginning of the war's third phase, during which ground activities in Lebanon were significantly upgraded. During this phase, toward the war's end, Israel planned to knock out the short-term rockets through a large-scale ground operation directed at Hezbollah's operational core south of the Litani River. During this phase, Israel's territory was hit by 2,080 rockets (an average of 160 daily), and twenty-three civilians and eighty-four soldiers were killed (of the eighty-four soldiers, thirty-three were killed during the war's final two days).

On August 9, the security cabinet approved a significant IDF ground maneuver in Lebanon. At the same time, diplomatic contacts continued in the hope of a political-diplomatic solution, and on August 10, Israel and the United States agreed on a text for a Security Council resolution calling for a ceasefire.

On August 11, at 16:40, while the Security Council was discussing the issue, the prime minister approved a large-scale ground operation in South Lebanon, which began at 21:00 as the Security Council members were finalizing the text of the resolution calling for a ceasefire.

On August 12, the ground operation continued. During the operation, an Israeli helicopter was shot down by Hezbollah. At 03:00 (Israeli time), the UN Security Council unanimously approved Resolution 1701, which called for a cessation of hostilities and the dispatching of 15,000 armed UN soldiers to South Lebanon. The next day, Israel announced that it accepted the resolution. This meant the termination of the ground maneuver without accomplishing all of its goals. Indeed, the United Nations announced that the ceasefire would come into force on August 14 at 08:00. The fighting continued up to that point in South Lebanon. During the day, the Israeli air force shot down two Hezbollah drones that were on an offensive mission. That night, the air force staged its last raid on the Dahiya quarter.

During the next few weeks, both the ceasefire and the aerial and naval blockade on Lebanon were maintained. The territories captured by the IDF were gradually handed over to UNIFIL, the United Nations force in Lebanon. On September 7–8, the aerial and naval blockades were removed, and IDF forces left Lebanon on October 1.

A TEN-YEAR RETROSPECTIVE

Ten years after the conclusion of Second Lebanon War, the Israeli evaluation of its significance and outcome has been modified. In its immediate aftermath and over the next few years, the dominant opinion in Israel was that the war was a failure. Israel's air force failed to put an end to the rocket attacks, which continued at the same pace throughout the war. The late and awkward employment of ground maneuver left a bitter taste. The Israeli public was affected by the discrepancy between its leadership's statements at the war's outset and the war's actual course and ending. The Israeli consensus held that Israel had failed in its war and that its deterrence had been significantly hurt. But with the passage of time, another version emerged, arguing that deterrence was reinforced, as demonstrated by Hezbollah's failure to act against Israel with minor exceptions since the summer of 2006.

Hezbollah's carefulness was motivated most of this time by the lessons its own leadership drew from the 2006 war. While

Israeli public opinion was busy looking at the war's negative aspects as seen from Tel Aviv and Jerusalem, Hezbollah looked at the damages it sustained and the limits of its ability to inflict massive damages on Israel. Consequently, even when offensive actions attributed to Israel took place after 2006, such as the 2008 killing of Hezbollah's most senior military leader, Imad Mughniyah, and Israeli attacks on convoys bringing military equipment from Syria to Lebanon, Hezbollah's response was limited. Since 2011, Hezbollah's conduct vis-à-vis Israel has been shaped primarily by the caution of its Iranian patrons as well as by a new development, its role in the Syrian civil war. This development will be analyzed below along with the other components of the "second wave" of massive changes in Israel's regional environment.

THE GAZA CHALLENGE

The Gaza Strip had long presented major challenges to Israel's political and military leadership. Any Israeli plan for resolving the Palestinian issue, be it the negotiations with Jordan's King Abdullah in the early 1950s or the peace process of the 1990s, had to cope with the lack of contiguity between the West Bank and the Gaza Strip. Population in the Gaza Strip grew dramatically over the years (it is close to two million at present), turning it into one of the world's densest and poorest areas, fertile ground for the growth of fundamentalist and other radical groups.

In 2005, Ariel Sharon decided to unilaterally withdraw from Gaza, evacuating the Israeli settlements and pulling out the

IDF. Sharon's decision had been preceded by a dramatic change in rhetoric. In the preceding decades, as a Likud politician and cabinet member, Sharon had led Israel's radical right wing and was seen as the principal architect and benefactor of the settlement project in the West Bank and the Gaza Strip. As prime minister, he underwent a profound change and began to speak about the ills of occupation and the inability to sustain it over time. Sharon's change of mind is still a debated issue between those who believe that it was a genuine change of heart by an older politician who became a statesman looking at historic responsibility and his own legacy, and those who believe that he was motivated by much less noble considerations. Whatever the motivation, Sharon made bold decisions at the grand strategy level. Sharon did not believe a negotiated solution with the Palestinians was feasible, and he decided to consolidate Israel's territory through unilateral action. He managed to fully extricate Israel from Gaza and, had he not been defeated by his own body, would probably have continued, on a more limited scale, in the West Bank.

Sharon's action was impressive in its boldness, but it was implemented in less than perfect fashion. Among other things, he failed to fully coordinate with the Palestinian Authority and its new leader, Mahmoud Abbas (Abu Mazen), who succeeded Arafat after the latter's death in November 2004. The political situation in the West Bank and the Gaza Strip in the aftermath of Israel's withdrawal was compounded by pressure on Sharon from President George W. Bush to allow free elections in the Palestinian Authority. Bush was motivated by his determination to demonstrate that the US invasion of Iraq in 2003 had laid the groundwork for the spread of democracy in the Arab world. The elections held in the Palestinian Authority in early 2006 ended with a clear Hamas victory. A Palestinian unity government was formed under the Hamas leader, Ismail Haniyeh, but Palestinian unity was a mirage. The conflict between Fatah and Hamas was intensified, and in mid-June 2007, Hamas staged a coup and took over the Gaza Strip. The president of the Palestinian Authority, Mahmoud Abbas, dismantled the unity government and outlawed Hamas and its armed units. Gaza became an independent entity controlled by Hamas.

Hamas was thus transformed from a movement and a terrorist organization into a political entity in control of territory. Its armed units were consolidated and converted into military units with their own military doctrine. Hamas was supported and inspired by Iran and Hezbollah. Between 2007 and 2009, Iran smuggled into the Gaza Strip large quantities of military equipment, mostly short-range (between twenty and forty kilometers) rockets and antitank missiles, and provided technological expertise that enabled Hamas to build explosive charges similar to those used by Hezbollah in Lebanon. Hundreds of militants left the Gaza Strip for advanced training in Iran, Syria, and Lebanon. Thousands of new recruits underwent military training in the Gaza Strip. As a result of these developments, Israel now confronted a new hostile entity on its southern borders. On a different level, it also confronted Iran, already present on its northern border, in the Gaza Strip.

Rockets and mortars launched from the Gaza Strip into Israel began on a small scale with the outbreak of the intifada in 2000. They continued during the following years. With the passage of time, primitive rockets became more powerful and acquired a longer range, which eventually reached central and northern Israel.

THREE MILITARY CAMPAIGNS (2008–2014)

In the span of six years, Israel found itself launching three military campaigns against Hamas in the Gaza Strip. These campaigns illustrated the complex relationship between conducting standoff operations through the use of airpower and firepower and relying on ground forces maneuver. They also illustrated the difficulty of conducting military operations in a densely populated urban environment and the challenge of adapting traditional laws of war to the current realities of warfare. The difficulties inherent in setting political goals for a military campaign conducted by a coalition government were exacerbated by profound disagreements in Israel regarding the future of the Gaza Strip and Hamas's control of this stretch of land.

The lessons Israelis had drawn from the war in Lebanon just two years earlier led to the development of a military strategy predicated on the concept of inflicting "painful damage" on Hamas to induce it to stop the rocket and mortar attacks and, more importantly, to delay the next round of fighting. The air force and firepower assumed primary roles, but ground forces were also integrated in the overall effort, a lesson from the Lebanon War. The chief targets were Hamas's essential resources (rockets and, later, underground tunnels) and its command-and-control systems. Israel systematically aimed to hit these targets to bring a swift end to the fighting and leave a lasting impression.

Operation Cast Lead

The damage and difficulties sustained by the population of Israel's southern coastline and the northern Negev due to Hamas rocket attacks since 2000 peaked in 2008. Several clashes occurred between Hamas and the IDF during that year, most severely in December. In the aftermath of a clash during which several fighters were killed, Hamas kept launching rockets and firing mortar shells into Israel's territory. On December 24, 2008, more than sixty rockets were launched. Three days later Prime Minister Olmert launched Operation Cast Lead.

Hamas's defensive plan had been prepared with the help of Iran and Hezbollah. It was predicated on the idea of maximizing IDF casualties by minimizing fighting in open areas and channeling it to densely populated, built-up urban areas. In these areas the plan was that the IDF would run into explosive charges and be hit by snipers, antitank rockets, and suicide bombers. Hamas also improved its techniques of concealing fighters in underground tunnels and among the civilian population. It continued launching rockets into Israel during the operation and using Israeli and international media to undermine the campaign's legitimacy. A lesson Hamas drew from the Lebanon War led it to assume that its ability to continue rocket attacks through the campaign would frustrate the Israelis and convince them that once again the IDF had failed to meet the expectations of the government and the public.

Operation Cast Lead was inaugurated on December 27 with a wave of massive bombings by air force jets and helicopters. During the first phase, about one hundred Hamas personnel were killed, most in a raid on a graduation ceremony held in a Hamas police school. About a week later, a limited ground operation was launched, and then expanded a bit during the campaign's third week. A total of 1,066 Palestinians were killed, most of them fighters for Hamas and smaller Palestinian organizations.

Hamas failed to emerge from the 2008 confrontation with achievements comparable to those obtained by Hezbollah in 2006. Israel sustained relatively few casualties (ten soldiers and three civilians) and limited damage. The IDF performed a successful ground maneuver into Gaza and inflicted several hundred casualties on Hamas.

Operation Cast Lead was conducted within an unusual international context: over the Christmas vacation and during the transition from the Bush to the Obama administrations. It was clear that Israel was constrained by the need to conclude the operation before the January 20 inauguration.

But the operation's conclusion was delayed by disagreements in the top echelons of the Israeli government. These disagreements in turn reflected the absence of a definitive solution to Israel's Gaza and Hamas dilemmas. While Prime Minister Olmert believed the operation should be concluded with a UN resolution comparable to the one that had ended the Lebanon War, his foreign minister (and party colleague), Tzipi Livni, argued for ending the campaign unilaterally, taking advantage of the renewed deterrence it had produced. Defense minister Ehud Barak (a coalition partner) advocated ending the operation with written understandings made directly with Hamas through Egyptian mediation. Finally, after twenty-two days of fighting, Israel announced a unilateral ceasefire, and the IDF began a gradual departure from the Gaza Strip. At the same time, Egypt's president, Husni Mubarak, hosted an international conference in Sharm el-Sheikh. The conference failed, as could be predicted, to produce a substantive solution to or improvement in the fundamental problem of Gaza, but it offered an opportunity for the participating European leaders to call upon Olmert in a display of diplomatic support. Early on January 21, a few hours after Barack Obama's inauguration, the IDF completed its withdrawal from Gaza.

The European leaders' display of support was soon overshadowed by the decision of the UN Human Rights Council to appoint a commission headed by the South African Jewish judge Richard Goldstone to investigate human rights violations by both parties. The commission's very appointment, the mandate it was given, and its makeup clearly illustrated the difficulties confronting Israel in its conflict with such enemies as Hamas and Hezbollah.

The commission's main finding was that both parties had acted systematically and deliberately against civilian populations, thereby violating the laws of war, which require belligerents to distinguish between warriors and civilians and to conduct their military activity in a manner designed to minimize civilian losses. The Goldstone report's bottom line was that both parties

were guilty of violating the laws of war and possibly of perpetrating crimes against humanity.

The Mavi Marmara *Affair*

In May 2010, a major incident reflected the significance of yet
another change in Israel's strategic environment: the quest of
Turkey's Islamist government to play a leading role in Middle
Eastern politics and its support for Hamas and its domain
in Gaza. In the 1990s Israel and Turkey had a close strategic
alliance. During the first decade of the new century, as Prime
Minister Recep Tayyip Erdoğan consolidated his rule, the alliance was replaced by enmity. Prime Minister Olmert was able
to contain the bad feelings by letting Turkey serve as a mediator between Israel and Syria, but the collapse of that mediation
and the launching of Operation Cast Lead shortly after Olmert's
return from a visit to Ankara produced a full-blown crisis.
Erdoğan was critical of Israel's Palestinian policy and particularly of its siege of Gaza. Israel had departed from Gaza but
maintained a naval blockade to reduce if not eliminate the
smuggling of weapon systems and other materiel from Iran. In
May 2010 a flotilla of six Turkish ships left for Gaza with the
stated mission of breaking the siege and bringing humanitarian
supplies. It was presumably organized by a Turkish Islamist
NGO, IHH Humanitarian Relief Foundation, a group closely
affiliated with Erdoğan's party, and clearly operated with the
government's blessing. Israel's navy stopped the flotilla en
route, acting beyond Israel's territorial waters. As Israel's naval
commandos took over the largest ship, the *Mavi Marmara*, it

encountered stiff resistance from armed men stationed on the ship. Nine Turkish nationals were killed. The Turkish-Israeli crisis was severely exacerbated. At one point Turkey threatened to dispatch its navy to Gaza, raising the prospect of a large-scale encounter between the two countries. The threat did not materialize, and during the past five years progress has been achieved in the effort to normalize Turkish-Israeli relations. Turkey's demand to be given a special position in Gaza has been one of the main obstacles to the conclusion of this effort. The issue was finally resolved in 2016, when Erdoğan, facing serious domestic problems and having sustained a series of foreign policy failures, decided it was time to end the crisis.

Operation Pillar of Fire

In response to renewed rocket attacks from the Gaza Strip, Israel, now led by Benjamin Netanyahu, launched Operation Pillar of Fire in November 2012. It was a relatively short operation lasting from November 14 to November 21. There was no ground forces movement into the Gaza Strip, and the bulk of the operation was conducted by the air force. The operation began with a surprising aerial raid that killed Ahmed al-Jabari, the de facto commander of Hamas's military arm. During the operation, Israel conducted thousands of raids against Hamas targets; Hamas in turn launched 1,500 rockets into Israel. It was the first time that Hamas was able to aim its rockets at cities in central Israel, including Jerusalem and Tel Aviv. Some 150 Gazans, most of them members of

Hamas and smaller Palestinian groups, were killed. In Israel, four civilians and two soldiers were killed.

The operation's swift end was the result of effective Egyptian mediation. Egypt was then ruled by Mohamed Morsi's Muslim Brotherhood government. The Islamist takeover in Egypt had a complex effect on Hamas's position in Gaza. As the Palestinian branch of the Muslim Brotherhood, Hamas enjoyed a significant improvement in its relationship with Egypt, better access to and from the Gaza Strip, and an overall sense of empowerment. This sense of empowerment derived also from Hamas's view of itself as part of "the green [Islamist] wave," which seemed to sweep the region after the collapse of the "Arab Spring." These were not welcome developments from Israel's perspective, but Egypt's increased influence over Hamas and its effectiveness as a mediator provided a silver lining.

The operation was concluded with a series of written understandings that were never implemented. This failure left Hamas frustrated and profoundly suspicious of Israeli intentions. In any event, the truce and calm collapsed after several months, and rocket attacks into Israel resumed, albeit on a smaller scale.

Operation Protective Edge

Israel's third large operation in the Gaza Strip took place against the backdrop of fresh changes in its strategic environment. The overthrow of Morsi's Egyptian government and its replacement by General Sisi's semi-military rule removed an important mainstay of Hamas's position in Gaza. Morsi's regime had viewed

Hamas as an extension of the Muslim Brotherhood and an accomplice of the jihadi offensive in the Sinai Peninsula. Hamas's reliance on Iran became controversial as Iran loomed in the Sunni world as the chief protector of an Alawite-Shiite Syrian regime butchering its Sunni opponents. Hamas was still supported by Qatar and Turkey, but its overall position had clearly diminished.

In June 2014 three Israeli youths were kidnapped and killed by a Hamas squad in the West Bank. Netanyahu's government responded with a massive campaign against Hamas infrastructure in the West Bank. Rocket fire from the Gaza Strip intensified, partly in response to this pressure and partly by rogue Palestinian groups. Israel responded by launching an operation that lasted fifty days, from July 8 to August 26, 2014. It ended with yet another ceasefire.

In military terms, the most significant initiative taken by Hamas prior to the operation was to construct an extensive system of offensive tunnels to allow dozens of fighters to enter Israeli territory. Hamas had concluded that without penetrating into Israel, it would be difficult to inflict the pain required for reaching "a significant achievement." Hamas was also successful in expanding its arsenal of rockets. It came to possess thousands of rockets with a range of forty kilometers and hundreds of rockets with a range of eighty kilometers.

In the end, both efforts met with limited success. The tunnels became a major issue in the Israeli debate on Gaza; Israel sustained casualties during fighting in the tunnels, but the strategic impact of, say, a raid on an Israeli village was not achieved. Some 4,500 rockets were fired at Israel during the campaign, but some fell in empty areas, and most of those aimed at urban areas were intercepted by the effective Iron Dome system, which had been developed with the support and close collaboration of the United States. Yet its large and diverse arsenal of rockets enabled Hamas to keep launching rockets into Israel, thus demonstrating its staying power. And while Israel coped successfully with the medium- and long-range rockets, it was hard put to deal with the short-range rockets and mortars, which inflicted damage and casualties along the border and led to a large-scale evacuation of civilian population. In these respects, echoes of the Lebanon War resonated during Operation Protective Edge.

There were two other significant dimensions to the operation. One had to do with the government's definition of the operation's goals and the strategy chosen by the IDF to implement them. It was hardly surprising that given the absence of clear political directives and profound disagreements in the cabinet, the IDF was hard put to craft a coherent strategy and implement it.

The IDF started the operation with a strategy similar to that employed in Operation Pillar of Fire, but when it became apparent that Hamas was uninterested in or incapable of ending the fighting, Israel adopted a different approach, seeking to force Hamas through attrition to end the confrontation without any achievements, formal or informal. Indeed, as the fighting dragged on, the Hamas leadership realized that it could expect no achievement beyond demonstrating its staying power, and agreed to a ceasefire.

During its first phase, the campaign consisted mainly of massive bombing by the Israeli Air Force. In defensive terms,

Israel had to cope with rocket attacks and with Hamas's efforts to penetrate Israeli territory from the sea or through the tunnels. In the second phase, which began on July 17, IDF ground forces entered the Gaza Strip to destroy Hamas's tunnel system. During the third phase, which began on August 5, the IDF's ground forces pulled out of the Gaza Strip, but fighting continued along the pattern established in the first phase. In the course of the campaign, twelve attempts were made to effect a ceasefire. Most of them were accepted by Israel and rejected by Hamas. It took fifty days to bring both parties to accept a ceasefire (which they have by and large adhered to during the past two years).

During the operation, the IDF attacked some six thousand targets in the Gaza Strip. It was the decision to topple high-rise buildings that may have persuaded Hamas to seek an end to the fighting. But the massive destruction exacted a high diplomatic price from Israel. Israel's Palestinian policy had been undermining its legitimacy for years; in this context, the third Gaza War and the destruction it entailed had a particularly devastating effect on Israel's standing in international public opinion. On the Israeli side, sixty-seven soldiers and five civilians were killed. Some two thousand Palestinians were killed, more than half of them combatants.

A second negative aspect was the bickering inside the Israeli cabinet. Prime Minister Netanyahu and defense minister Moshe Ya'alon were guided by a desire to minimize IDF casualties and refused to establish the destruction of Hamas as the war's aim. As they saw it, if Israel were to destroy Hamas, it would have to assume control of and responsibility for Gaza.

But two cabinet members to their right, Naftali Bennett and Avigdor Lieberman, tried to promote such a policy and were openly critical of the war's conduct. The Netanyahu-Ya'alon policy of seeking a period of calm was uninspiring, but the Bennett-Lieberman policy made little sense. All told, Israel remained without attractive policy options with regard to Gaza.

4

THE ARAB SPRING AND THE ARAB TURMOIL: A NEW MIDDLE EASTERN REALITY

The wave of massive changes that reshaped the Middle Eastern arena in the early years of the new century was followed, starting in December 2010, by two additional waves: the Arab Spring (2010–11) and the Arab Turmoil (2011 to the present). The Arab Spring was the term given to a series of popular rebellions against authoritarian regimes in the Arab world that began in Tunisia in December 2010 and spread to Egypt, Yemen, Bahrain, Libya, and Syria. The toppling of the authoritarian regimes of Ben Ali in Tunisia and Mubarak in Egypt by young rebels using social media and seeking democracy was initially seen as a potential turning point toward the massive change, leading to reform and democracy, that the Arab world and the world in general have been expecting for decades. By the second half of 2011, the optimism generated in the Arab world and elsewhere was dashed by the grim realities of what came to be known as the Arab Turmoil. Tunisia was the only country to witness a fairly successful transition from dictatorship to a more democratic form of governance. Elsewhere the reformist movement was checked by force (Bahrain) or led to an Islamist takeover followed by the reestablishment of a semi-military regime (Egypt) or to civil war and anarchy (Syria, Libya, and Yemen). In several monarchies, the regimes skillfully initiated reforms and other measures that enabled them to survive the revolutionary wave.

For Israel, the Arab Spring and the Arab Turmoil presented different challenges. A number of Israeli politicians welcomed the prospect of a transition to democracy in much of the Arab world. A durable peace, it was argued, could be made and maintained only with democratic partners. But this was a minority view. The government and most analysts were primarily concerned with the threat to Israel's peace treaties with Egypt and Jordan. Since 1979 and 1994, respectively, peaceful relationships with Egypt and Jordan had been pillars of Israel's national security. The formation of Morsi's Islamist government in Egypt and the threat to the stability of the Hashemite regime in Jordan raised grave concerns in Israel.

The Arab Spring also exacerbated the debate over the Palestinian issue in Israel and between Netanyahu's government and the Obama administration. The advocates of an Israeli-Palestinian agreement warned that the revolutionary wave was likely to affect Palestinians in the West Bank, sweep away the pragmatic leadership of the Palestinian Authority, and possibly lead to a new intifada. Such scenarios, they argued, should be preempted by resuming a serious peace process. Similar arguments were made by the Obama administration, already exasperated by what Obama and his team saw as a negative Israeli approach to the issue. Obama in fact framed his position in a broader context. He was enthused by the Arab Spring and tried to persuade Netanyahu that Israel should place itself "on the right side of history." Netanyahu was not persuaded. He was dubious about the prospects of genuine democratization in the Arab world. From his perspective, it would be perilous for Israel to make territorial or other concessions during a period of instability.

These debates were, however, overshadowed in short order by the changing trends in the Middle East. The Palestinian issue did not vanish as one of Israel's most crucial issues, but its prominence in regional and international agendas diminished as new issues, the Syrian civil war in particular, came to the fore.

By 2014 a very different regional arena had crystallized around Israel. It was defined by the following major issues:

1) The Arab crisis. Several Arab states could be defined as failed states (Syria, Iraq, Lebanon, Sudan, Libya, and Yemen). With regard to two of them, Syria and Iraq, the very future of the state in its current boundaries was in question. Under the rubric of the end of Sykes Picot (a code name for the colonial post–World War I peace settlement), the future of the Arab state system was introduced into regional and international discourse on Middle Eastern politics. The sense of Arab weakness and crisis was exacerbated by the domestic problems in Egypt and Saudi Arabia, the Arab world's two most influential states. In Egypt the Muslim Brotherhood government headed by Mohamed Morsi, which had emerged from the post-Mubarak elections, was toppled in late 2013 by a combination of popular resistance and military coup and replaced by the semi-military regime of General Abdul Fattah al-Sisi,

who was elected president in 2014. Sisi consolidated his hold over the country, but he confronted, on top of its massive socio-economic problems, an Islamist challenge (the Muslim Brotherhood, many of whose members had gone underground but were still entrenched in the country) and a jihadi challenge, the latter primarily in the Sinai Peninsula. The jihadis in Sinai established a branch of the Islamic State and operated to some extent in cooperation with like-minded groups in Gaza. They launched occasional attacks on Israeli targets, but their main efforts were directed at Egyptian military and governmental targets.

In Saudi Arabia the old and ailing King Abdullah died and was succeeded in January 2015 by Salman, another octogenarian. Salman is the last of Ibn Sa'ud's sons to hold the throne and clearly a transitional figure. Much of his power has been invested in his son Mohammad, who pursues aggressive regional policies atypical of Saudi Arabia's traditional, low-profile, careful style. Mohammad Bin Salman's persona and style are the focal point of an intense struggle for influence within the royal family that hampers Saudi Arabia's efforts to shape Arab politics according to its priorities and interests.

2) The Syrian civil war. The Syrian crisis that erupted in March 2011 has exacted an unprecedented price from the country's population (more than 400,000 dead, a larger number maimed and wounded, and half the population—11 out of 22 million—displaced, more than 4 million as external refugees and the rest domestic ones). The crisis has unfolded on three levels: domestic (pitting the regime of Bashar al-Assad against a very diverse opposition), regional (a conflict between Assad's

main supporter, Iran, and its regional rivals, headed by Saudi Arabia), and international (between Russia and its Western rivals, headed by the United States). The regime has managed to maintain a semblance of sovereignty in Damascus and about 40 percent of the national territory, while a variety of groups and local militias—jihadi, Islamist, and secular—control the rest of the country. The most effective of these groups is the Islamic State in Iraq and Syria (ISIS). As its full name implies, ISIS began as the Iraqi branch of al-Qaeda, then shifted its focus to Syria, fighting on behalf of the Sunni majority against an Alawite-Shiite regime. It came to control a large swath of land on both sides of the nonexistent Iraqi-Syrian border. Eventually ISIS established a quasi-state, announced the formation of a caliphate, and chose the Syrian city of Raqqa as its capital. At the present time (summer 2016), Assad's regime is conducting, with Russian help, a major offensive against ISIS, in an effort to regain control of a significant portion of its territory. On Syria's northeastern edge, the bulk of the fighting is conducted between ISIS and Kurdish militias. Media coverage of the war and policy debates have raised the prospect of Syria's partition, formal or informal, into several statelets and the possibility of Alawite secession.

One important dimension of the Syrian crisis is the issue of chemical weapons. Under Bashar al-Assad's father, Hafez, Syria had built a chemical arsenal as part of its deterrent capacity against Israel. In 2012 reports began to emerge that such weapons were being used against Syria's own population. Against that backdrop, President Obama stated that the use of chemical weapons by the Syrian regime would be for him "a red line and a game changer." When massive use of chemical weapons against civilians near Damascus was reported and verified in August 2013, the Obama administration was confronted with a major dilemma. The president was determined to avoid significant military involvement in Syria but also aware of the damage that failure to respect his own "red line" would inflict on Washington's and his own credibility in the Middle East and elsewhere. He authorized a punitive air strike, only to cancel it soon thereafter. He was saved from total humiliation by Vladimir Putin, who offered a deal: Syria would surrender and destroy its chemical arsenal in return for a US decision not to attack. The deal was endorsed by the UN Security Council in September and implemented (almost fully) over the following few months. It was an important event in three respects: 1) It demonstrated Russia's increased relevance and influence in the region, particularly in Syria. 2) It underscored Washington's "pivot" away from the Middle East. 3) It reduced the risk to Israel from Syria's chemical arsenal. By the end of 2016, with Russian and Iranian help, the Assad regime has regained the initiative but the crisis was still far from being over.

3) The rise of ISIS. The organization has had an important role in the Syrian context, but its origins are in Iraq. Its swift transformation from one jihadi militia fighting in the Syrian civil war into a force threatening the very foundations of the Iraqi state occurred in June 2014, when it captured the large city of Mosul in northern Iraq and advanced on Baghdad. For a while it also seemed to threaten Jordan. This success can be explained by the collaboration between the original al-Qaeda in Iraq and elements from Saddam Hussein's army and security services who had been ousted by the American invasion in

2003 and later participated in the Sunni insurrection against the United States. More broadly, the organization represented, at least to some extent, Iraq's 20 percent Sunni population, who had been estranged by al-Maliki's Shiite-dominated regime. The organization had been supported early on by other Sunnis in the region, who saw it as a tool in their conflict with the "Shiite Crescent." It also had a complex relationship with Turkey and Assad's regime, whose policies regarding ISIS combined conflict and cooperation. Later on, particularly after establishing a caliphate and a proto-state on both sides of the Syrian-Iraqi border, the organization replaced al-Qaeda as the chief instrument of global jihad. It established effective franchises in such places as Libya, the Sinai, and Equatorial Africa. Most important were the thousands of European citizens who came to Syria and Iraq to be trained and fight. These recruits became the nucleus of a significant terrorist threat in France and Belgium. This threat led several European countries to change their outlook on the Syrian civil war, now regarding Assad and his regime as preferable to ISIS. The terrorist threat to Europe soon became affiliated with the massive immigration of refugees, primarily from Syria, which shook the foundations of the European Union. Developments in such Middle Eastern countries as Iraq and Syria thus became urgent European and global issues.

4) The Iranian nuclear issue. Iran's quest for a nuclear weapon has already been mentioned. In October 2003, negotiations began between Iran and European foreign ministers. The United States joined in formally during George W. Bush's second term, but the negotiations failed to produce results for several years. In 2010–12, the threat of an Israeli aerial raid

against Iran's nuclear installations hovered in the air. In March 2013, secret bilateral negotiations between the United States and Iran began in Oman, leading to the temporary and permanent agreements of 2014 and 2015. These agreements postponed the threat of an Iranian nuclear breakout for at least ten years but failed to deal with other dimensions of Iran's aggressive foreign and regional policies.

5) The Saudi-Iranian, Sunni-Shiite, rivalry. The American-Iranian agreement was criticized by such US allies as Saudi Arabia, which view Iran as the gravest threat to regional stability. They point to Iran's role in the Syrian civil war and in Iraq, to its use of Hezbollah as a tool in Lebanon, Syria, and other locations, to its agitation in Yemen and Bahrain, and to its renewed relationship with Hamas. The Saudis and other Sunnis regard this conflict in denominational terms, as a Shiite-Sunni conflict; Jordan's King Abdullah coined the term "the Shiite Crescent," referring to the axis stretching from Tehran via Iraq and Syria to the Mediterranean. For Sunni regimes, Iran's role in the Syrian civil war—as Assad's main supporter in the war, using Hezbollah and Shiite volunteers or recruits from Iraq and Afghanistan in support of an Alawite (Shiite sectarian) regime—is reason enough for concern. Saudi Arabia was suspicious of President Obama and his administration. They regard him as sympathetic to Iran and its regime and are fully aware of his criticism of their policies in the region. It is important to note that there is not a single Sunni bloc opposing Iran in the Middle East. Saudi Arabia and Egypt are hostile to the Muslim Brotherhood, while Turkey and Qatar are supportive of the organization and its orientation. This split

has hampered the Sunni effort to topple Bashar al-Assad in Syria and has also influenced the response to events in Gaza, where Hamas is perceived as an extension of the Muslim Brotherhood.

6) New American and Russian policies. The Obama administration used the term "pivoting" to describe its choice to allocate less significance to the Middle East and greater importance to the Asia-Pacific region in the conduct of its foreign and national security policies. This concept must not be interpreted in sweeping terms. The United States continues to have important interests in the Middle East and has invested significant effort in conducting negotiations with Iran, in trying to manage its exit from Iraq and Afghanistan, and for the last several years, in renewing serious negotiations between Israel and the Palestinians. But President Obama made a clear decision to avoid further massive military involvement in the Middle East. He reduced America's military presence and activity in Iraq and Afghanistan to a bare minimum and refused to assume a military role in the Syrian crisis. The United States leads the military campaign against ISIS, but it tries to do so by relying on the military forces of other countries and actors (such as Syrian and Iraqi Kurds). The impact of this policy has been amplified by Obama's open criticism of traditional US allies in the region, by his treatment of Husni Mubarak during the Egyptian uprising, and by his explicit overruling of his foreign policy establishment, which supported a greater US role in Syria.

The vacuum thus created offered a golden opportunity to Vladimir Putin. His earlier role in Syria was dramatically enhanced by his decision to send his air force to Syria in the fall of 2015 and to take an active role in the civil war. Under the guise of fighting the Islamic State, Russia's air force bombed Assad's more moderate rivals and civilian targets in northern Syria. Putin made the decision to intervene to help Assad at a critical moment, when rebel forces were threatening his core areas, but also in order to display Russia's new influence in the region. Russia's aerial presence in Syria created fresh problems for both Turkey and Israel. Turkey shot down two Russian jet fighters operating on the border area between Turkey and Syria, triggering a major crisis in its relationship with Russia. Israel has coordinated its aerial activity over Syria with Russia and so far has avoided unwanted collisions, but its activity in Syria is thus hampered. More broadly, having Russia as a military neighbor is a problem for both Turkey and Israel.

7) Turkey's role. One important by-product of the Syrian crisis has been the unveiling of several structural weaknesses in the Turkish state. During Erdoğan's first years in power, Turkey loomed as a would-be regional hegemon. Relying on its large population, strong economy, imperial tradition, and large military force, Erdoğan's Turkey tried to compensate for its rejection by Europe by building its influence in neighboring areas: the Caucasus, Central Asia, and primarily, the Arab world. This policy met with increasing difficulties, most importantly in the Syrian context. Prior to the civil war, Erdoğan tried to act as Bashar al-Assad's mentor, but afterward turned against him. As an Islamist leader, he projected himself as the supporter of Syria's Sunnis. As a neighboring country, Turkey absorbed a large number of Syrian refugees, provided supply

routes for weapons and other aid to rebel groups, and offered political and operational headquarters for the Syrian opposition. But Turkey's Syrian policy was obstructed by domestic opposition and the Kurdish problem. Turkey had built a reasonably good relationship with the Iraqi Kurds but was suspicious of the Syrian Kurds and their affiliation with the radical Kurdish opposition in Turkey. Turkey's Kurds are estimated at 20 percent of the population, and Erdoğan and many other Turks are concerned that Kurdish sovereignty across its borders with Iraq and Syria would encourage secessionism. On several occasions, Turkey was willing to collaborate with ISIS to weaken the Kurds. As had been mentioned, Turkey is also deeply concerned with Russia's military role in Syria. For Turkey, the Syrian refugees in its territory are both a problem and a tool to be used in its relationship with Europe.

8) Kurdish resurgence. As has been mentioned, in the Turkish, Iraqi, and Syrian contexts, one by-product of the Arab Turmoil has been a resurgence of the Kurdish issue. The Kurds were one of the original victims of the post–World War I settlement in the Middle East. They were denied statehood and divided among four states—Turkey, Iran, Iraq, and Syria—and became minorities in all four. During most of the twentieth century, it was the Turkish republic's policy to suppress and ignore the Kurdish issue: Kurds were referred to in Turkey as "Mountain Turks." This policy changed over time, and the Turkish state eventually recognized the reality of a Kurdish minority of some 20 percent. The consequences varied. Periods of violent conflict with the radical element among the Turkish Kurds were replaced by efforts to integrate the Kurds peacefully

into Turkish national life. Turkey was concerned in the 1990s by the autonomy gained by Iraq's Kurds after the First Gulf War, but in time a modus vivendi was established, predicated on the Kurdish leadership understanding that they must not cross the line separating autonomy from sovereignty. The US invasion of Iraq in 2003 led to a further enhancement of Kurdish autonomy and power in northern Iraq, and the Syrian civil war resulted in the emergence of virtual Kurdish autonomy in northeastern Syria. The Kurds in Iraq and Syria emerged as the most effective local force fighting the Islamic State. These developments have worried Erdoğan's Turkey. He has been concerned by the prospect of a Kurdish decision to cross that line in Iraq and particularly by the empowerment in Syria of the Kurdish group known as PYD, which is affiliated with the radical PKK in Turkey. These concerns led to the collapse of Erdoğan's dialogue with the Kurdish opposition in Turkey and played a major role in his decision to sometimes collaborate with ISIS.

ISRAEL'S IMMEDIATE RESPONSE

So far, the repercussions of these developments for Israel and its responses have been limited. Israel has increased its cooperation with Egypt and Jordan and has improved its tacit relationship with the Gulf states, but its main preoccupation has been the Syrian civil war. Ironically, of Syria's five neighboring states, Israel has been the least involved in—and the least affected by—the Syrian civil war.

Between 1948 and 1992, Syria was Israel's most bitter Arab enemy and, after the signing of the Egyptian-Israeli peace accord, its most formidable military foe. Since 1992, and until the eve of the outbreak of the Syrian civil war in March 2011, the two countries have been engaged in an intermittent peace process as well as an ongoing conflict. Syria, along with Iran, supported Hezbollah and conducted a war by proxy against Israel in Lebanon. In 2007, Israel discovered that North Korea was secretly building a nuclear reactor for Syria and destroyed it in September of that year.

Needless to say, the future of the Syrian regime and the Syrian state are crucial issues from Israel's point of view. As the strongest military power in the region, Israel could affect the course of the Syrian civil war, but it has chosen to adopt a modest role. Following the outbreak of the civil war, two schools of thought crystallized in the Israeli leadership and community of experts. The first, sometimes known as the "devil we know" school, has argued that as problematic as Bashar al-Assad and his regime are, they are preferable to an Islamist or jihadist alternative. The second maintains that the Russian-Iranian-Assad-Hezbollah axis presents a more serious threat to Israel's national security, as the 2006 war in Lebanon demonstrated. In any event, this remains an academic debate since the Israeli government has decided that its ability to affect the course of events in Syria is limited and could produce more problems than benefits. Thus, Israel has concluded that supporting the opposition would play into the regime's hands. The al-Assad regime insists that the Syrian civil war is not a genuine rebellion but a conspiracy hatched from the outside by such actors as the United States and Israel. Israeli support for the relatively moderate rebels would then be exploited by the regime to delegitimize them as "Israeli agents."

Netanyahu's government chose to stay on the sidelines, offer humanitarian aid, and intervene only when the ceasefire line in the Golan was affected or when weapons of mass destruction and other sophisticated weapons fell into terrorist hands. In practice this is meant cultivating a working relationship with opposition groups on the Syrian side of the ceasefire line and conducting several aerial raids against convoys transferring sophisticated weapons from Syrian depots to Hezbollah.

Russia's military intervention in Syria in the fall of 2015 has complicated Israel's calculus. Israel is uncomfortable with Russia's military presence in Syria and the limits it imposes on the Israeli Air Force's freedom of activity in Syria's airspace. In the context of pursuing a closer relationship with Putin's Russia (an important element in Netanyahu's foreign policy), Israel has invested special effort in coordinating aerial activity over Syria so as to avoid incidents similar to the one that occurred between Syria and Turkey.

Another by-product of the development described above has been the improvement of Israeli-Turkish relations. Erdoğan's regional ambitions and pro-Hamas policies brought the two former allies to the verge of a collision, but as Turkey's regional policy encountered growing difficulties, Erdoğan began to take a different view of his relationship with Israel. This has paved the way for reconciliation and normalization of the bilateral relationship.

THE IDF'S RESPONSE TO THE
NEW REGIONAL ORDER

We have just described Israel's response to some of the changes that have taken place in the region. These responses were based on decisions made on a case-by-case basis rather than as part of a comprehensive strategy in response to the far-reaching changes in Israel's strategic environment. So far the only comprehensive approach in Israel has been formulated by the IDF. Given the history of the past sixty-eight years, it is hardly surprising that the IDF rather than other organs of the Israeli government has responded in a comprehensive way to the massive changes in the Middle East and that the IDF's response was not limited to pure military strategy but has also dealt with the larger political issues.

About ten years after the publication of chief of staff Dan Halutz's document, which was shelved after the Second Lebanon War, the IDF again tried to write a conceptual document on the strategic level. This time it was chief of staff Gadi Eizenkot who published a document titled *The IDF Strategy* (this was an unclassified version of the confidential original, prepared for public consumption). It was the first document under such a title ever published by the IDF. Even though the document did not follow a political directive or a written national security concept, it positioned itself as "the keystone for force buildup and operation." This document provides an impressive, though not problem-free, effort to formulate how the IDF perceives its operational environment, the threats against which it might act, and the current strategy for building the force and using it in response to a variety of threats.

The document describes three types of threats:

1) States, both distant (Iran) and near (Lebanon and Syria), described in the document as "failed" and "in process of disintegration"
2) Substate organizations such as Hezbollah and Hamas
3) Terrorist organizations not linked to a particular state or community, such as ISIS

The document reflects a clear concept of the change in the threats faced by the IDF. It emphasizes the decline of the threat from regular armies and the exacerbation of the threat from substate organizations, irregular or semiregular. It also emphasizes the increased threat to the home front as well as the effort to present a strategic threat to the national vulnerable points and the Israeli economy and the tendency of Israel's enemies to deploy and merge into populated civilian areas.

The document adopts a traditional Israeli concept according to which Israel is engaged in a conflict that can still be evaluated as "insoluble," and is therefore required to maintain overtime a strong military force possessed of offensive capability and concepts in order to implement a defensive security policy. The document emphasizes the quest for long periods of security calm and the need to create effective deterrence to achieve them. The document emphasizes also the importance of strategic cooperation (primarily with the United States), the need to strengthen Israel's position in the regional arena, the importance

of obtaining legitimacy for the employment of force when necessary, and the need to preserve the IDF's qualitative edge in
advanced weapons.

The document describes three potential political targets for
military force:

1) Postponing the next confrontation through the employment of force as a matter of routine
2) Preserving a strategic position or improving it once the
   enemy has launched violent activity
3) A radical transformation of the current position to the
   point of neutralizing actors or effecting substantial
   changes in their potential or position

With regard to employing force as a matter of routine, the
document contains an interesting innovation that reflects developments which have occurred in the IDF during the last few
years. In the aftermath of the Second Lebanon War, the IDF
recognized the need to emphasize constant readiness for war.
The IDF adopted the outlook that an army is always in one
of two positions: war or preparation for war. This Clausewit-
zian principle suited the IDF's traditional distinction between
current security (employing force for different tasks, mostly on
the borders, in peacetime) and employment of force in war.
Departing from this basic distinction, Chief of Staff Eizenkot
described an ongoing activity initiated by the IDF on a systemic
scale that takes place between wars in order to delay the next
war and produce better conditions for employing force should
it break out. According to the document, this activity is designed

to weaken enemies, to limit their buildup of forces, and to deny the legitimacy of their activity. This is to be achieved through both secret and public operations of a multidisciplinary nature that combine military activity with measures taken in the media and in the economic, legal, and political domains. It seems that this is the conceptual basis for a series of operations attributed to Israel in the international media, particularly in the Syrian and Lebanese contexts, including the destruction of the Syrian nuclear reactor in 2007, the killing of Imad Mughniyah in 2008, and the ongoing effort to prevent Syria from transferring weapon systems to Lebanon since 2013.

With regard to the employment of force during fighting, the document provides a conceptual basis for the type of operations in which the IDF has been involved in the last decade. It describes two essentially different kinds of potential demand at the political level:

1) The demand to achieve a full and clear military defeat of the hostile organization
2) The demand to damage the enemy in a limited, well-defined fashion

As for the first type, the document adopts the position that the IDF should strive for victory, such that either a ceasefire or a political settlement can be forced on the enemy by ensuring either its military defeat or its inability and unwillingness to continue fighting. These can be achieved by denying capabilities, by destroying enemy forces, by limiting their effectiveness against the Israeli home front, by reaching targets the enemy sees as vital, and by weakening its will to continue fighting.

The novelty of the document can be found in its description of how force can be used in the second type of conflict, defined as "a limited campaign." According to the document, the IDF would be employed in such missions to partially incapacitate specific enemy capabilities, significantly damage strategically important targets and governmental institutions relevant to the war effort, limit effectiveness against the Israeli home front, and restrain enemy decisions on using particular weapons or methods.

Another innovation is the attention paid to confrontations defined as counterfire against Islamic substate organizations. According to the document, in such conflicts the IDF will be required to end the confrontation with a victory and to dictate the terms for ending the war, to significantly limit damage to the home front, to shape a better security environment in the war's aftermath that will prevent rebuilding the enemy's military potential, and to preserve legitimacy for force employment.

With regard to the operational concept, the document describes a powerful multidimensional employment of force aimed at achieving a swift decision through simultaneous, multidimensional employment of force combining precision and ground maneuver (as a crucial component) against all dimensions of the hostile system, which would throw that system out of balance, disrupt its normal operation, and prevent it from functioning as a fighting system. In this respect, the document seems to break away from the way force was employed in recent campaigns, in which the IDF was guided by the concept of erosion. Even when not explicitly formulated as such, this approach viewed the erosion of the enemy's force as its guiding line. Thus the IDF employed increasing firepower to erode the enemy's capabilities and operational infrastructure. This approach exacted a cost from the Israeli home front because fighting continued as long as the enemy kept its capacity to fire rockets and missiles. By contrast, the Eizenkot document describes a substantially different approach: the IDF—in response to provocation—will inflict on the enemy an immediate, simultaneous, combined blow. The document allocates an important role in this updated concept to ground maneuver. Its role would be to penetrate enemy territory swiftly in order to affect governmental survivability and destroy the military infrastructure. Fire is directed simultaneously against thousands of targets, both planned and targets of opportunity. These operations are supported by special operations, cyber operations, qualitative intelligence, and effective defense against enemy fire.

As reflected in the public version of the Eizenkot document, the IDF's current operational concept seems to include the following components:

- A continuous campaign of deterrence to prevent the exacerbation of threats before this can be implemented. Such a campaign in times of routine is primarily directed at preventing the delivery of unique weapon systems, potential game changers, or hitting key figures in the enemy's ranks and deterring them from carrying out particular operations.

- An effort in both collection and research aimed at building an intelligence infrastructure, which is key to dealing with an enemy attempting to hide in the environment. Such an infrastructure should expose the enemy and facilitate attacks on crucial points.

- Employing force in a manner that emphasizes the relative advantages of a regular army possessed of high firepower and improved maneuverability. What is intended is the simultaneous, multidimensional employment force combining precise fire and ground maneuver (as a crucial element) against all dimensions of the enemy system so as to throw it out of balance, disrupt its normal activity, and prevent it from functioning as a fighting system.

- An effort to shorten the duration of the fighting, primarily to limit damage to the Israeli home front. But it should be borne in mind that given developments on the other side, the ability to shorten the campaign is limited, as recent confrontations have shown.

- Responding to the needs of the population both in the war zone and on the home front.

- Effective public relations and media campaigns that contend successfully with the media campaign of the other side and protect domestic and external legitimacy.

Undoubtedly the publication of the Eizenkot document was an important milestone in the evolution of Israeli strategic thinking. For the first time, the Israeli public was presented with a coherent conceptual infrastructure regarding the IDF's concept of its operational environment, its mission, and the preferred mode of employing force against a variety of threats. Like the Halutz document of 2006, it reflects the IDF's attempt to cope with these issues in the absence of a clear strategic framework comparable to the one offered to the US military by the documents published by the president and the secretary of defense.

The document was released to the Israeli public in August 2015. Less than a month later, in September 2016, Israel found itself contending with a novel type of terror. The Eizenkot document is unlikely to provide the conceptual tools for dealing with this new terror, which involved individuals, "lone wolves," as a rule (but not exclusively) youngsters unaffiliated with organizations (some of them had belonged to Palestinian organizations in past years or had been involved in security violations) who had been inspired to act by social networks or the media. They attacked in most cases with knives and in some cases with improvised or standard weapons. Between September 2015 and mid-2016, hundreds of such acts took place, leading to the deaths of dozens of Israelis. By April 2016 a decline in the level of activity was noticeable, though several deadly acts (including a shooting at a Tel Aviv entertainment center) were perpetrated subsequently.

In certain respects, this wave of terror is part of a global phenomenon of "lone wolves" devoid of clear organizational affiliation who have committed deadly acts in various parts of the globe (France, Belgium, Denmark, Turkey, the United States, and several locations in Asia and Africa). Some of these acts were clearly inspired by the Islamic State (though the perpetrators had not been members of the organization or joined it only while perpetrating their attacks).

The terror wave's proximity to the publication of the Eizenkot document was, of course, purely coincidental, but it underlines the fact that the document sought to describe a response to the threats that Israel had been confronting in the past few decades rather than dealing with the implications of the new operational environment. The document offers an impressive summary of Israeli approaches to the repercussions of the earlier turmoil in the Middle East, which gave rise to the "new generation of enemies" and the hybrid wars of the last two decades. The major confrontations between Israel and that generation of enemies, which we have described here, produced a fairly coherent response that is clear in the Eizenkot document. This response may well be relevant for future confrontations with Hezbollah or Hamas but not necessarily for the current turmoil.

The potential repercussions of the current turmoil have yet to be clarified. We know from experience that such a process takes time. But it is clear now that Israel is facing several new operational and strategic challenges. For one thing, Syria's unraveling and Iran's and Hezbollah's involvement in the Syrian civil war and the prospect of Assad's survival could lead a new front to emerge in the confrontation with Hezbollah and could reshape that confrontation. The presence in the Sinai of elements affiliated with ISIS has already led to a number of attacks and could develop into an active front. The wave of "terror by individuals" could be an early symptom of a novel phenomenon that Israel would have to deal with in the coming year: the formation of groups of individuals, not necessarily shaped like the large Palestinian organizations, operating mostly through social networks to carry out terrorist attacks. Finally, as Operation Protective Edge in Gaza showed in 2014, the new structure of regional politics can have an important impact on the conduct of future military operations.

THREE LEVELS OF ISRAELI STRATEGY AND SECURITY POLICY

It is hardly surprising that the IDF, through the Eizenkot document, is the only organ of the Israeli government that has formulated a comprehensive approach to the massive changes in the Middle East and their impact on Israel's national security. As described in the first section of this monograph, the three levels of national strategy and security policy that have crystallized in the United States do not really exist in the Israeli context. During its early days, the Israeli state had a leader with the capacity and determination to formulate a grand strategy, who dominated the security and military establishments through the force of his personality and intellect. In later years, Israel's national strategy and security policies have been formulated and implemented through the interplay between the cabinet level and the IDF leadership. The manner and quality of the cabinet's performance in the conduct of national security policy has varied greatly over the years. Ben Gurion's successor, Levi Eshkol, followed in his footsteps in holding the security portfolio. But he lacked Ben Gurion's command of defense and military matters, and the authoritative chief of staff of the IDF became a de facto minister of defense. This division of labor collapsed during the crisis that led to the Six-Day War in 1967. For the next six and a half years, a former chief of staff of the IDF and a dominant charismatic figure, Moshe Dayan, served as minister of defense, acting as a rule with an authoritative prime minister, Golda Meir. Their failure in October 1973 brought Rabin to power in May 1974. Rabin had to offer the defense portfolio to his rival, Shimon Peres, and their rivalry had a negative impact on defense policy. During the next forty years, similar patterns were followed. Three prime ministers— Rabin in his second term and Ehud Barak, both former chiefs of staff of the IDF (and Rabin a former minister of defense as well), along with Shimon Peres in 1995–96—also held the defense portfolio. Other prime ministers, including Menachem Begin in his second term, Benjamin Netanyahu, Ariel Sharon, and Ehud Olmert, deposited the defense portfolio with a party or a coalition partner. The quality of their collaboration has varied. The dual or triple axis of prime minister, minister of defense, and chief of staff of the IDF has been the crucial component in the making of national security policy.

While the IDF has both a tradition and the instruments for strategic planning, the cabinet level lacks either. The National Security Council, which operates alongside the prime minister, was never empowered or equipped to perform these tasks, nor does the ministry of defense have the requisite tools. Although it has a political-military division, its tasks are different and it certainly does not deal with strategic planning. Formulating a national strategy requires a rare combination of routine diligence (such as the publication of periodic reports) with the ability to respond quickly to significant changes in the strategic environment. Overall, Israel's record during the past sixty-eight years in responding to the security threats and in employing military force in the service of government policy has been impressive, but these achievements were not the result of either a correct structure or a sound process.

The interaction between the cabinet level and the IDF leadership has been tested severely during the recent campaigns in Lebanon and Gaza, as the IDF had to act in the absence of clear political aims defined by the cabinet. Within the cabinet, a forum crystallized after 2001, known as the "security/political cabinet." It is predicated on a formal decision in 2001 to form a ministerial committee for security affairs and has been vested with the power to assist or restrain the prime minister in making national security policy. Currently with a minister of defense (Avigdor Lieberman, a coalition partner and political rival) and the radical minister of education (Naftali Bennett) in his security/political cabinet, Netanyahu's freedom of action has been significantly curtailed.

Netanyahu and his cabinet need to deal with Israel's current regional environment on two levels. One can be defined as comprehensive: the quest, as Netanyahu described it, "to create foci of stability" around Israel. One focus would be the close but discreet security cooperation with Egypt and Jordan. A second is the normalization with Turkey (prior to the coup attempt in that country). A third is the close relationship developed with Greece and Cyprus during the tension with Turkey. A fourth is the more amorphous relationship with the Sunni bloc in the

Middle East, most significantly Egypt, Jordan, Saudi Arabia, and some of the Gulf states. These states as a bloc, and each of them separately, have had good reasons for upgrading their relationship with Israel. Countries like Saudi Arabia and other Gulf states are primarily preoccupied with the Iranian threat, the threat of jihadi terrorism, and their unhappiness with the policies of the Obama administration. Against that backdrop, Israel has loomed as an important partner. For Egypt—facing the threat of terrorism in the Sinai and Hamas's affiliation with the Muslim Brotherhood in Gaza—and for Jordan, contending with domestic and external threats, collaboration with Israel has been essential. The Sunni bloc's identification with and support for the Palestinian cause has declined but remains a significant constraint, particularly in the age of social networks and satellite television, which magnify the impact of public opinion. Consequently, their willingness to cooperate with Israel is limited to tactical cooperation, mostly behind the scenes. A significant upgrade of Israel's relationship with the Sunni Arabs to the point of actually forming a pragmatic bloc in the region cannot be envisaged before launching a new Israeli policy toward the Palestinian issue.

The most important issue shared by Israel and the Sunni Arab states is concern with Iran's nuclear and regional ambitions. The nuclear agreement with Iran did not deal with Iran's regional ambitions and subversive activities. Saudi Arabia and the Gulf states, Iran's immediate neighbors, feel threatened and exposed by its policies in Iraq, Yemen, Bahrain, and Saudi Arabia's own Eastern Province. Israel is concerned with Iran's overall posture in the region and the prospect that it will renew its quest for nuclear military capability. Israel seeks to curtail Iran's nuclear ambitions, assuming that the Iranian leadership will resume the quest for a nuclear arsenal openly at the end of the period designated by the agreement or surreptitiously prior to that time. It will continue to invest a massive intelligence effort in monitoring Iran's nuclear plans and is keeping alive the option of resorting to a military option. Israel's acquisition of F-35 planes is the most explicit indication of Israeli thinking and planning in this regard.

The other prominent issues on the cabinet's security agenda are the ongoing civil war in Syria, Hezbollah's arsenal in Lebanon, and Hamas's arsenal in Gaza. As we have seen above, Israel has managed so far to maintain a low profile in the Syrian crisis, but this could change rapidly, and Israel could find itself involved in the crisis or facing an ominous challenge from Iran, the Assad regime, and Hezbollah or active hostility from jihadi groups in southern Syria. Another confrontation with Hamas or Hezbollah could erupt. As we have seen, IDF strategy is currently focused on this prospect, but the IDF does not deal with the political aims to be pursued by Israel in either case. Netanyahu's decision in June 2016 to replace Defense Minister Ya'alon with Avigdor Lieberman, in addition to its domestic political dimension, could have far-reaching implications for Israel's national security policy. Lieberman reinforces the hardliners in Netanyahu's government and early on voiced his views on a number of national security matters. Most significantly, he announced that the next war with Hamas in Gaza, if there is one, will be the last. In 2014, as foreign minister, Lieberman advocated toppling the Hamas government in Gaza as the proper war aim for Israel (in contradistinction to Netanyahu and Ya'alon's policy of containment). His more recent statement suggests that in the event of another military confrontation with Hamas, he will advocate that position from the more influential position of minister of defense.

Beyond these immediate issues lies Israel's lingering inability since 1967 to formulate a national consensus on the future of the West Bank and the larger Palestinian issue as the keystone for formulating an updated grand strategy. At this point Israel is governed by a purely right-wing government whose members support either maintaining the status quo (which means creeping annexation) or a proactive policy of annexation. Netanyahu belongs to the first group. His unstated policy is an updated version of the Iron Wall: by standing fast, Israel has brought the Arab states to accept its existence; by holding on to the same passive steadfastness, it will eventually defeat Palestinian nationalism as well. This view is sharply contested by groups and individuals in the center Left of the Israeli political spectrum but is not effectively manifested by the mainstream opposition.

SOURCE NOTES

Chapter 2

1. Hassan Nasrallah, speech broadcast on al-Manar TV, February 22, 2008.

2. Quoted in Itamar Rabinovich's forthcoming biography of Yitzhak Rabin (New Haven, CT: Yale University Press, 2017).

3. Yossi Peled, "Israel's Operational Concept: Is a Change Really Necessary?" [in Hebrew], *Maarachot* 318 (February 1993), p. 5.

4. Amnon Lipkin Shahak, speech delivered in Jerusalem, November 1, 1998.

5. Moshe (Chicco) Tamir, *A War without a Medal* [in Hebrew] (Tel Aviv: Maarachot, 2005), p. 193.

6. Ibid., p. 272.

7. Wesley K. Clark, *Waging Modern War: Bosnia, Kosovo, and the Future of Combat* (New York: Public Affairs, 2001).

Chapter 3

1. Interview with J5 MG Shlomo Yanai (IDF [in Hebrew]), *Armour*, October 1999, p. 8.

2. Ehud Olmert, speech at the Institute for National Security Studies conference, Tel Aviv, July 12, 2012. Reproduced in *INSS Military and Strategy*, April 2014.

BIBLIOGRAPHY

Ben Gurion, David. "The Military and the State" [in Hebrew]. *Maarachot,* nos. 279–80 (1981): 2–11.

Ben Yisrael, Yitzhak. *Israel's National Security Doctrine* [in Hebrew]. Tel Aviv: Misrad ha-Bitachon, Universita Meshuderet, 2013.

Brun, Itai. "'While You're Busy Making Other Plans': The 'Other RMA.'" *Journal of Strategic Studies* 33, no. 4 (2010): 535–65.

Brun, Itai. "But Where Is the Maneuver?" [in Hebrew]. *Maarachot* (2008): 420–21.

Clark, Wesley K. *Waging Modern War: Bosnia, Kosovo, and the Future of Combat.* New York: Public Affairs, 2001.

Dror, Yehezkel. *A Statecraft-Security Israeli-Jewish View of the Chief-of-Staff's Document "The IDF Strategy"* [in Hebrew]. Jerusalem: Jewish People Institute, 2016.

Eizenkot, Gadi. *The IDF Strategy* [in Hebrew]. Tel Aviv: IDF Chief of the General Staff, 2015.

Halberstam, David. *War in a Time of Peace: Bush, Clinton, and the Generals.* New York: Touchstone, 2001.

Levite, Ariel. *Offense and Defense in Israeli Military Doctrine* [in Hebrew]. Tel Aviv: Hakibbutz Hameuchad, 1988.

Luttwak, Edward N. *Strategy: The Logic of War and Peace.* Cambridge, MA: Harvard University Press, 2001.

Olmert, Ehud. Speech at the Institute for National Security Studies conference, Tel Aviv, on July 12, 2012. Reproduced in *INSS Military and Strategy*, April 2014.

Peled, Yossi. "Israel's Operational Concept: Is a Change Really Necessary?" [in Hebrew]. *Maarachot* 318 (February 1993).

Rabinovich, Itamar. *Israel and the Changing Middle East.* Washington, DC: Brookings Institution, 2015.

Shelach, Ofer. *Dare to Win: A Security Policy for Israel* [in Hebrew]. Tel Aviv: Miskal-Yedioth Ahronoth and Chemed Books, 2015.

Tal, Israel. *National Security: The Few against the Many* [in Hebrew]. Tel Aviv: Dvir Publishing House, 1966.

Tamari, Dov, and Meir Klifi. "The IDF's Operational Concept" [in Hebrew]. *Maarachot* 423 (2009).

Tamir, Moshe. *A War without a Medal* [in Hebrew]. Tel Aviv: Maarachot, 2005.

Winograd Commission. *The Final Report of the Commission to Investigate the Lebanon Campaign in 2006* [in Hebrew]. Tel Aviv, 2008.

Itai Brun

Brigadier General (Res.) Itai Brun served as the head of Israel Defense Intelligence (IDI) Analysis Division from June 2011 to January 2015. In this position he provided ongoing intelligence assessments to the senior military leadership (the Chief of General staff) and the political level (the Prime Minister, the Defense Minister, and the Cabinet).

Prior to this position, he was the head of the Analysis Department in the Israeli Air Force Intelligence and the first director of the Israeli Defense Forces' DADO Center for Interdisciplinary Military Studies. He founded the center in late 2006, after the second Lebanon War, and served as its director till January 2011.

Brun is a lawyer and was admitted to the Israeli Bar in 1996. His academic background includes law and political science. He earned his LL.B degree (law studies) from Haifa University (cum laude) and a Master's Degree in Political Science (Diplomacy and Security Studies) from Tel Aviv University (cum laude). Brun is also a graduate of the Israeli Defense Forces' Command and Staff College.

Brun has published several publications on intelligence and air power issues. His book *Intelligence Analysis—Understanding Reality in Time of Dramatic Changes* (2015) was published (in Hebrew) by the Israel Intelligence Heritage and Commemoration Center (IICC).

Itamar Rabinovich

Professor Itamar Rabinovich is the founding president of the Israel Institute (Washington and Tel Aviv), Deputy Chair of the INSS (Institute of National Security Studies) affiliated with Tel Aviv University, Global Distinguished Professor at New York University, and Non-Resident Distinguished Fellow at the Brookings Institution.

From 1992 to 1996 he served as Israel's ambassador to Washington and chief negotiator with Syria, and from 1999 to 2007 served as president of Tel Aviv University, where he is now a professor emeritus of Middle Eastern history.

He is the author of several books and numerous essays on the contemporary history and politics of the Middle East, among them *Syria under the Ba'th, 1963–66: The Army-Party Symbiosis, The War for Lebanon, 1970–1985, The View from Damascus: State, Political Community, and Foreign Relations in Twentieth-Century Syria,* and *The Lingering Conflict: Israel, the Arabs, and the Middle East, 1948–2012.* His biography of Yitzhak Rabin will be published by Yale University Press in 2017.

HERBERT AND JANE DWIGHT
WORKING GROUP ON
ISLAMISM AND THE
INTERNATIONAL ORDER

INDEX

A Belfast GIRL

"This is a beautiful book to be read with all senses open.
We are drawn by living language into a feast of stories.
Maggi Peirce's life in Ireland before and after World War II
provides a poignant and profound experience. Each chapter
is written with an immediacy of presence and a tenderness
of appreciation. This is a storyteller's coming of age, from
another place and time that renders the reader more human."

LAURA SIMMS
Storyteller and author of *Our Secret Territory: The Essence of Storytelling*

*The author, aged 17, appears at the left in
this photo that includes her sister, Dot.*